INSIDE CANADIAN FORCES TRANSFORMATION:

INSTITUTIONAL LEADERSHIP AS A CATALYST FOR CHANGE

MICHAEL K. JEFFERY, CMM, CD
LIEUTENANT-GENERAL (RETIRED)

CANADIAN DEFENCE ACADEMY PRESS

Canadian Defence Academy Press
PO Box 17000 Stn Forces
Kingston, Ontario   K7K 7B4

Produced for the Canadian Defence Academy Press
by 17 Wing Winnipeg Publishing Office.
WPO30499

Library and Archives Canada Cataloguing in Publication

Jeffery, Michael K., 1947-
Inside Canadian Forces transformation : institutional leadership as a catalyst for change / Michael K. Jeffery.

"Produced for the Canadian Defence Academy Press by 17 Wing Winnipeg Publishing Office"--T.p. verso.
"WP030499"--T.p. verso.
Issued by: Canadian Defence Academy.
Includes bibliographical references and index.
ISBN 978-1-100-13768-1 (bound). -- ISBN 978-1-100-13766-7 (pbk.)
Cat. no.: D2-254/2-2009E (bound). -- Cat. no.: D2-254/1-2009E (pbk.)

1. Canada--Armed Forces--Management. 2. Organizational change --Management.
3. Leadership. 4. Command of troops. I. Canadian Defence Academy II. Canada.
Canadian Armed Forces. Wing, 17 III. Title.

UB210 J44 2009   355.30971   C2009-980331-3

Printed in Canada.

3 5 7 9 10 8 6 4 2

TABLE OF CONTENTS

FOREWORD

For more than four years, since the appointment of General Rick Hillier as Chief of the Defence Staff (CDS) in early 2005, transformation has been an overriding and consistent theme for the Canadian military. As leader of one of the four CDS Action Teams and later as Chief of Staff of the Canadian Forces (CF) Transformation Team, I was intimately involved in many aspects of the Transformation. Barely ten years after the dark years of the mid-1990s and the Somalia Inquiry, a charismatic military leader was proposing a bold new vision of the CF, one that was intended to reshape the Canadian military institution for the 21st century. There was a wave of vibrant optimism with *this* Transformation that generated unparalleled passion and much-needed confidence. It was a period unseen in recent memory.

This book, *Inside Canadian Forces Transformation: Institutional Leadership as a Catalyst for Change*, authored by former Chief of the Land Staff, Lieutenant-General (LGen) Michael Jeffery, is the first comprehensive analysis of the CF Transformation. It addresses the challenges that CDS General Hillier (2005-2008) and his CF leaders faced as they attempted to restructure and transform this institution. The book benefits greatly from the experiences and perspectives of an author who, as the most senior leader of the Canadian army, had initiated his own transformation of that institution a few years earlier. LGen Jeffery accessed current sources and key CF Transformation documentation in the preparation of his manuscript; more importantly, however, he interviewed many key senior leaders, both military and civilian, who were involved in or touched by the CF Transformation.

To be effective, any institution requires substantial congruence between the competence of its leaders and the relevance of its *raison d'être*. Fifteen years ago, the CF initiated an extensive review of its post-Cold War competence and effectiveness of its leadership and professionalism. To address the leadership side of leadership-institution congruence, the Canadian Defence Academy (CDA) was established with a mandate to research, redefine and generate significant education and development to equip the CF with highly effective leaders for the 21st century. While the CDA continues to enhance the leadership and professionalism of its members, the focus has expanded in recent years to include the other side

FOREWORD

of leadership-institution congruence, to examine the appropriateness of its institutional direction, strategic practices, operational effectiveness, and organizational structure.

The expectation of the CDS of 2005 was for a commitment from his military leaders, with their renewed professionalism and enhanced leadership capacities, for institutional reformation through a formal *CF Transformation* initiative. His military leaders were to support this timely Forces-wide transformation through a controlled evolution of review and restructuring. The CDS, on retirement in 2008, was satisfied that much of this evolution had been successful. He had left his mark on the institution.

In this book, LGen Jeffery lays out the sequence of CF initiatives, compares them to textbook models of institutional change, and describes the strengths and weaknesses of this real-world, practical transformation of the Canadian military. He assesses whether the CF, as a large and complex organization, has done so successfully. LGen Jeffery's observations and conclusions are most informative.

I recommend this book to all leaders responsible for initiating important change and leading transformational processes of any magnitude. I recommend that it be used as a case study for leaders to explore and to analyze the lessons to be learned from such an applied transformation. *Inside Canadian Forces Transformation: Institutional Leadership as a Catalyst for Change* provides guidance, and wisdom, not only to military change leaders but, as well, to change agents in other government ministries, non-government organizations, private industry and academe. Having been part of the CF Transformation team for nearly one year, I will admit that I do not agree with all the conclusions of LGen Jeffery. That being said, I have the utmost respect for LGen Jeffery's objectivity and balance in reviewing these years of CF Transformation, and I urge you to read this book and take on board the many lessons and insights he offers in his excellent analysis. It is a timely must-read for all responsible and conscientious leaders, military or non-military, as this challenging 21st century unfolds.

Major-General Daniel Gosselin
Commander, Canadian Defence Academy

PREFACE

The year 2005 marked the appointment within the Canadian Forces of the new Chief of the Defence Staff, General Rick Hillier, a leader who assumed command with an enthusiastic dedication to restructuring and transforming the Canadian military institution. He remained committed to this mission throughout his tenure, until his retirement in 2008. *Inside Canadian Forces Transformation: Institutional Leadership as a Catalyst for Change* examines the experiences of, and lessons identified by, Canadian military leaders and others participating in this multi-year initiative of institutional reformation.

This book, contracted by the Canadian Defence Academy's Canadian Forces Leadership Institute (CFLI), is a timely Canadian Defence Academy Press publication for the professional development of Canadian military leaders. The mission of CFLI is to generate and disseminate research, concept development and doctrine on military leadership, command and the profession of arms, all to support the generation of effective military leaders. This CFLI mission, of necessity, includes the presentation and publication of diverse, informed perspectives from qualified authors. This book provides one such perspective.

For the last decade of the 20th century, military institutions around the world experienced major post-Cold War, global, national, societal and internal pressures for change, for increased internal accountability, and for overdue restructuring and reorganization, all aimed at greater mission success. In the eyes of the CDS, this mission success, being influenced by such aspects as rapid technological innovation and the threatening global security environment, necessitated an aggressive approach to CF Transformation. This transformation demanded the integration of two elements: (1) the capacities of CF leaders being professionally enhanced, and continuing to be educated and trained in their professional competencies, over recent years sufficiently to master new and expanding national and global challenges; and (2) a revised CF orientation achievable through the examination and reformation of its strategic practices, operational direction and organizational mandate.

Extensive research had been conducted previously on leadership and professionalism by the CFLI, and then published in recent profession of arms and leadership manuals and books. Importantly, some of that research led to the approval by the CDS of a CF Professional Development Framework (PDF, also referred to, by 2008 in Canadian Forces Headquarters, as the Leadership Development Framework (LDF)) with its five requisite military leader element or metacompetencies – *Expertise, Cognitive Capacities, Social Capacities, Change Capacities*, and *Professional Ideology*. These five meta-competencies, cross-tabulated with four leader levels – junior, intermediate, advanced and senior – expanded upon the foundations of leadership and professionalism to be developed incrementally and progressively throughout the careers of CF leaders. In a time of CF Transformation, these leader capacities would be particularly challenged, a point made by the CDS as his CF transformation initiative commenced in 2005.

Fundamentally, then, the onset of the 21st century represented a time of profound challenge as the CF institution reconstituted itself while paying attention to the evolving profession imbedded within it, as well as expanding global threats, changing societies world-wide, and a technological revolution influencing military missions, all of these being issues for the CF Transformation. *Inside Canadian Forces Transformation: Institutional Leadership as a Catalyst for Change* is seen as part of the answer for leaders addressing this cluster of complex challenges. The book is authored by former Chief of the Land Staff, LGen Michael Jeffery. His foundational experiences included career-long military service from junior to senior leader levels, from operational levels to the most senior executive corporate levels, and from an early career of leading people to senior executive leadership of both people and the military institution. His experience is that of the top executive of an organization of over 30,000 members. He has overseen the responsibilities inherent in full stewardship of the profession of arms. LGen Jeffery, himself, has initiated strategic planning for institutional transformation and change, followed by leading and implementing that transformation through to completion. These qualifications and experiences gave him unique perspectives on institutional transformation that are reflected in this book. Through a combination of reputation, character, trust, respect, familiarity and professional associations, LGen Jeffery is a totally informed subject matter expert who thoroughly comprehends the dynamics of the years of CF Transformation. This book benefits greatly from his disciplined, factual and fair review.

All chapters in this book, as written by LGen Jeffery, reflect his experiences, research, interviews and assessments, and should be viewed as such. The book's contents do not represent CF doctrine or policy, however they do showcase the informed perspective of one knowledgeable and experienced senior Canadian military leader highly conversant with institutional transformation. His is a perspective offered to other CF leaders preparing for their own senior leader responsibilities. However, as expressed previously by Major-General Gosselin, Commander of the Canadian Defence Academy, *Inside Canadian Forces Transformation: Institutional Leadership as a Catalyst for Change* provides guidance not only to military change leaders, but also to many others. This book is recommended as a timely must-read for all conscientious and creative leaders engaged in organizational change and institutional transformation. For those leaders seeking additional information on transformation of institutions, a list of Selected Readings is provided at book's end.

Robert. W. Walker, CD, PhD
Canadian Forces Leadership Institute
Canadian Defence Academy

ACKNOWLEDGEMENTS

When I was first asked to undertake this project, I had little real understanding of the magnitude of the task and it has taken more time and effort than I ever anticipated. Had it not been in large part a labour of love, I doubt that the book would have been completed.

The reader of this work will rightfully question the validity of many of the perspectives presented here, and some commentary on my sources is warranted. During the project, I was given access to literally hundreds of documents recording the intent, direction, actions and concerns of the CF leadership throughout the period. While the full list of references is too extensive to be listed here, some of the most significant ones are identified under Selected Readings. However, the full complement is available from the Canadian Forces Leadership Institute.

This documentation was complemented by numerous discussions permitted by my wide access to the CF's senior leaders and key staff, both military and civilian. Time precluded me from speaking to all of the players involved in the process but, to ensure accuracy and balance, I endeavoured to glean the insights of a broad range of people. This saw over forty formal interviews, conducted on the basis of non-attribution, with those who were closely involved with the planning and implementation of transformation. There were also many more informal discussions with the CF's senior officers involved in all aspects of the CF's transformation efforts. Finally, I was given the opportunity to participate in a number of CF senior leader professional development sessions which provided me a unique insight into the dynamics of the CF general and flag officer team.

This book could not have been written without the support of many people. I am particularly grateful to the now-retired Chief of the Defence Staff, General Rick Hillier, for his generosity with his time and for providing his perspective on many of the strategic issues facing the CF. Many of the CF's currently serving and formerly serving generals and flag officers kindly provided their insights into the change dynamic. These were essential to understanding the various points of view and the institutional chemistry during this period. In addition, a number of the key senior National Defence Headquarters

ACKNOWLEDGEMENTS

(NDHQ) staff, intimately involved in the change process, provided their unique perspectives and were instrumental in balancing my analysis. They also were most helpful in reviewing early drafts of the book and their comments very much guided my thinking.

Finally, I must recognize the staff of the Canadian Forces Leadership Institute who originated the idea for this study and who were instrumental in bringing it to fruition. In particular, I wish to acknowledge the invaluable assistance and guidance of Dr. Robert W. (Bob) Walker, without whom this book would never have been completed.

The support I received in researching this subject and the insights I gained through the many discussions I had were critical to my understanding of the dynamics of transformation within the CF, but any errors, in fact or analysis, are mine alone.

As indicated in the introduction, this book is, at best, a superficial analysis of a complex and ongoing process. However, if it can in some small way assist the Canadian Forces leadership in their continual pursuit of improvement of the military institution in Canada, then the investment has been worth it.

Michael K. Jeffery

INTRODUCTION

Change is a constant in any organization. The emergence of new structures, the acquisition of new equipment with different capabilities, the adoption of new technology or the development of new processes or doctrines are normal evolutionary changes for any organization. But fundamental change is rare. Institutions, in particular military institutions, tend to be conservative and to eschew new directions that create turmoil and risk.

Fundamental change occurs for a variety of reasons: new threats, the emergence of disruptive technologies, new doctrine or concepts, and changing resource pressures, to name a few. However, historically, such pressures exist for some considerable time, without anything but minor organizational tinkering having occurred. Real change requires a catalyst, either a significant military event, usually a defeat, or the emergence of a leader with a new vision and the courage to implement it.

General Rick Hillier assumed command of the CF on 4 February 2005. He arrived with a vision for a very different CF, a "transformed" military institution that he commenced to implement immediately. What followed was the start of what may be the most significant change to the CF in over half a century.

INTENT

This work is a case study on institutional leadership during CF Transformation. It is focused on the CF institutional leader and is intended to act as a primer on change, to show how institutional leaders achieve real change, the challenges they face, and some of the techniques they use to overcome them. Equally, it will address the difficulties and failures encountered. It is a professional development treatise, not a report card on CF Transformation.

APPROACH

This case study is about the initial stage of CF institutional change during the 2005-2007 timeframe. It will provide an analysis of CF Transformation as an example of institutional leadership in action. It will also provide a chronology of events, describing in global terms the changes that were instituted, and will analyze those events to determine what worked and what did not. It will draw on this analysis to provide insight into the institutional leadership and change management lessons to be learned. It will then attempt to highlight the challenges that the CF will face, as it continues to transform.

As with all such studies, this one started with an extensive review of the available reference material on CF Transformation. This had its limitations, as the speed of implementation and the turmoil created by institutional change has resulted in a less than desirable record of events. However, this reference review was complemented by a large number of interviews and discussions undertaken at a number of levels with those involved in CF Transformation. The focus of these discussions was to understand what had occurred and why, that is to say, to obtain the various perspectives as a means of deducing what actually happened.

In building this case study, the CF manual, *Leadership in the Canadian Forces: Leading the Institution*, was used as the doctrinal foundation. This work was supplemented with references on change management theory, with the principal change reference being John Kotter's *Leading Change*.[1] This was selected primarily because it is the one favoured by General Hillier and generally in use within the CF. However, for ease of understanding, Chapter 2 of this book provides a summary of the fundamentals and principles of organizational change that form the theoretical foundations for this work.

It must be stressed that this is not an exhaustive work; rather it is a snapshot of a process that continues to evolve. Unlike the historic treatise that relies on major reference research and mature perspectives developed over the long term, this work has been time-constrained, relying on, at times, incomplete reference documents and the perspectives of those still living the change. As a consequence, the key factors that lead to change are not always as clear as they would be years after the fact. In addition, individual perceptions are greatly affected by the specific roles that people are playing and the positions they have taken on the changes being implemented.

This study is meant to be widely read and attempts have been made to frame it in a readable style. Additionally, a briefer version of this case study, titled "Inside CF Transformation", will appear in the *Canadian Military Journal*.[2] In this book, there has been limited use of jargon and a use of common acronyms only where such use facilitates understanding. In this vein, the male personal pronoun will be used throughout, vice an alternating approach or the more cumbersome he/she.

Finally, while many senior leaders within the CF, including the CDS, were generous with their time and perspectives, the views and analysis in this case study are mine. In this context, where commentary reflects the position of the CF, the CDS or other senior officers, that is because I have assessed it as such. It does not necessarily reflect CF policy or the opinions of any member of the CF.

CHAPTER 1

CONTEXT AND BACKGROUND

"There is nothing more difficult to carry out, nor more doubtful of success, nor more dangerous to handle, than to initiate a new order of things. For the reformer has enemies in all those who profit by the old order, and only lukewarm defenders in all those who would profit by the new order...[because of] the incredulity of mankind, who do not truly believe in anything new until they have had actual experience of it."

Nicolo Machiavelli, *The Prince*[3]

In order to understand the magnitude and importance of CF Transformation, it is vital to establish an understanding of what has gone before. The CF has not remained stagnant but has undergone a considerable number of changes over the years. It has instituted new strategies and policies as required by government direction, adapted its operational structure and doctrine as required by changing threats, and adopted new technology as the operational environment demands and resources permit. These many incremental changes were essential to creating the demand for more fundamental change and for setting the conditions that made CF Transformation possible.

THE COLD WAR

With the benefit of hindsight, it can be seen that the post-Second World War military in Canada was relatively stable. Humankind faced a bipolar world, where East-West confrontation was the dominant influence. This Cold War shaped every aspect of Canadian defence policy both at home and abroad. It meant a military focused on the Soviet threat and specialized to optimize Canada's contribution to the North Atlantic alliance. The navy concentrated on anti-submarine warfare, principally in the North Atlantic; the air force concerned itself with the nuclear strike role in Europe and the air defence role at home, as part of the North American Aerospace Defense Command (NORAD)[4]; while the army maintained a conventional mechanized infantry capability as part of the North Atlantic Treaty Organisation (NATO) defence on the central European front.

Unquestionably, change occurred during this period. New technology resulted in more modern platforms and capabilities, and changing government policy saw adjustments in overall military contributions and deployments. However, the nature of the threat and, as a consequence, the focus of military operations, was largely unchanged throughout that period, with little variance in the structure or culture of the CF.

Such stability existed despite significant international and domestic influences. The emergence of peacekeeping, and Canada's love affair with it, saw considerable military force deployed in support of the United Nations (UN). Indeed, Canada was, for a long time, one of the largest contributors to UN peacekeeping operations and for many years prided itself in being involved in every UN mission. However, as important as such missions were to the country and the development of a professional military leadership cadre, they were in reality a side show. The main act was to be performed on a Cold War stage.

At home, the 1964 White Paper articulated the intention to unify the Royal Canadian Navy, Canadian Army and Royal Canadian Air Force into the Canadian Armed Forces.[5] These major organizational changes, after the law passed in April 1967, became effective 1 February 1968, and had a profound impact on every aspect of the military. The Management Review Group's actions of 1971 subsequently led to the integration of the CF Headquarters with the Department of National Defence (DND), creating NDHQ. Indeed, the reorganization took fully 20 years for the tectonic shocks to subside and the institutional dust to settle from these changes. However, when it did, despite the reorganization of national command and control and the reformation of administration of the CF, the fighting arms were much as they had been. The navy, army and air force[6] of 1990, apart from their more modern equipment, would have been very much at home with the military of the Second World War or the Korean War.

1990-2005: THE EMERGING NEW WORLD ORDER

With the end of the Cold War, the Canadian government was looking for a peace dividend. Reductions to the defence budget began as early as 1990.

This trend accelerated significantly in 1994, as the government introduced a debt reduction financial strategy that included a major reduction to the defence budget. In objective terms, the defence budget declined from a high in 1993 of $12B to a low of $9.4B in 1998/99.[7] The impact on the CF of such a massive reduction was tremendous and included military base closures, major cuts in personnel, reduction of equipment fleets, and elimination of some capabilities. In short, it was a general shaving of the military ice cube. Every part of the institution was affected. This also saw the first major attempt at organizational change of the DND since integration of the headquarters in 1972 with the institution of a re-engineering effort under the Management Command and Control Re-Engineering Team (MCCRT).[8] This initiative's intent was to streamline the organization and administration of DND and the CF in order to improve efficiency while maintaining effectiveness. The aim was, quite literally, to achieve more with less. Paradoxically, as governments slashed defence, they also demanded more – as it turned out, much more – with serious consequences.

Arguably, the post-Cold War world started with the First Gulf War in 1991. After all, this was the first major conflict where the "east-west" balance was not a significant factor. While this event saw the introduction of some remarkable new technologies, it was not a new kind of conflict, but was conducted very much in the conventional mode of "industrial age" military operations.[9] However, it took place in a strategically vital region and the Soviet Union's limited influence on the decision to go to war is significant. Canada was one of the first nations to agree to condemn Iraq's invasion of Kuwait and it joined the United States-led coalition, contributing warships and CF-18 fighters. It did not contribute ground troops but did send some ground support personnel, including a Field Hospital.

In February 1992, Canadian "NATO-assigned" troops stationed in Germany deployed to the Balkans as part of the United Nations Protection Force (UNPROFOR). This was to become the first of many operational deployments in the region and arguably the first of the "new world order". Canada contributed a wide variety of capabilities through the almost decade-long commitment to the region, both under UN and NATO leadership. This included a significant ground commitment, a periodic naval presence in the Adriatic Sea and the Mediterranean Sea, and a commitment of airlift. It also saw the deployment of a number of CF-18s as part of NATO's Stabilization Force (SFOR) and participation in the Kosovo Air Campaign. This was not peacekeeping, and these operations saw some of the most intense activity and more fighting than Canadians had seen since Korea. But, neither was it the kind of operations planned for during the Cold War. Peace support operations, as they came to be known, were really operations to fight to establish peace.

This period was a sobering one for the CF. These operations revealed that, despite years spent in readiness for war on the central front, the CF's operational capabilities had, in a number of cases, declined significantly. While the standard of training was generally not in doubt, equipment shortcomings were serious. These ranged from weapon and communications limitations for the CF-18s and a lack of defensive suites for the CC-130s, to a broad range of protection limitations for the soldiers and the army's vehicles. While many of these problems were resolved, it took time – some would say too much time – during which the morale of the troops, in particular within the army, eroded. Inadequate personal protective equipment and the personal frustrations that came with literally having to share individual equipment left a sense amongst the troops that nobody cared. This view was exacerbated by the deplorable manner in which casualties, both physical and mental, were handled when personnel were repatriated.

Events of this timeframe also called into question the ethics and professionalism of the leadership. Most noteworthy was the "Somalia crisis" that became a flash point for concerns both within and outside of the CF. The main trigger for the crisis involved the Canadian Airborne Regiment, which was deployed to Somalia in late 1992 and early 1993, as part of the Unified Task Force (UNITAF). While largely a successful mission, it saw the torture and murder of a Somali youth by Canadian soldiers. This, and the subsequent management of the case by the military and political leadership, cast a spotlight on the mission and the CF that had serious political consequences for the CF and the country.

The government formed a Commission of Inquiry into the Deployment of Canadian Forces to Somalia, and the very public testimony before the Commission unleashed a torrent of pent-up frustration and concern. Normally stoic soldiers came forward to complain about their treatment in operations and upon deployment home, which led to other investigations and inquiries on a range of issues. It also saw the appearance of servicemen and women before the House of Commons Standing Committee on National Defence and Veterans Affairs (SCONDVA), and the condemnation of the military for its treatment of its personnel. Revelations on issues ranging from pay and housing to treatment of injured soldiers after release were almost daily fare. It was a very bleak period for the CF.

FACING THE PROBLEM

As a consequence of the evident problems and failures with the CF, the government ordered a number of investigations and took a variety of actions with respect to the CF, some internal to DND, some external. The key recommendations can be found in three influential reports; the findings of the *Commission of Inquiry into the Deployment of Canadian Forces to Somalia*, the recommendations of the House of Commons SCONDVA on the social and economic challenges facing members of the CF, and the recommendations of the Minister of National Defence in his *Report to the Prime Minister on the Leadership and Management of the Canadian Forces*. These three reports set in motion a wave of policy changes with respect to the CF on the critical issues of values, leadership, military justice and discipline. These policy changes resulted in a wide range of initiatives including, but not limited to:

- Enhancement of preparations for operational missions;

- Clarification of the lines of responsibility between military and civilian personnel;

- Improvement of the promotion and command selection system;

- The training and selection of leaders;

- Improvement of officer and non-commissioned member training, education and professional development;

- Elimination of some of the weaknesses of the army regimental system; and

- Improvements in informing the Canadian public about the CF.

This very difficult period for the CF has to be seen in some context. Unquestionably, the institution and its leadership failed during a very demanding period and the reforms imposed by government were long overdue. Lost in the public debate on professionalism, ethics and leadership, however, was recognition of the serious challenges faced by the CF. Foremost amongst these was the lack of resources essential to maintain a modern military. Imposition of a "peace dividend" and the massive cuts to the defence budget as part of government debt reduction placed an already fragile institution in serious jeopardy. In order to balance the ledger, the CF underwent a massive downsizing of the personnel base, cutting the regular military from 88,800 to 60,000 and the civilian work force from 36,600 to 20,000, a total loss of over 45,000 full-time personnel.[10] Not surprisingly, given the state of the institution and its low morale, this saw the departure of some of the military's best – resulting in a demographic problem, commonly referred to as the missing cohort, which continues to exist today.

In parallel with these reductions was the implementation of major re-engineering efforts under MCCRT. In an attempt to economize, every administrative activity and process used by DND and the CF was re-evaluated with a view to streamlining how business was conducted. While this initiative did not directly affect operational structures, it imposed significant change on every aspect of the CF and DND institutional structure (headquarters, bases, wings, and all parts of the training, personnel and support systems). Perhaps the greatest change was the closing of the "Command" headquarters[11] and the creation of the Environmental Chiefs of Staff (ECS) as commanders of their commands, situated within NDHQ.[12] The result was not only a loss of capacity, as personnel numbers dwindled, but turmoil in command and control as the guidelines and procedures for virtually every activity were changed – often with no notice and without full understanding of the implications. The result was an organization focused on efficiency vice effectiveness. Significantly, the approach accepted a high degree of risk and traditional government accountability measures were put into abeyance in order to achieve the change and reduction targets. Perhaps not surprisingly, given the magnitude and speed of change, many of the risks came due, which was to have serious consequences for the institution and resulted in many positive changes being undone.

Throughout this period, the CF also faced an extremely high operational tempo, demanding more output from an institution under great strain. Understandably, this strain was not uniform as the demand for skills varied with the mission. But, in general, the capabilities that faced the greatest load were naval crews, helicopter and transport aircraft crews, army manoeuvre units, in particular infantry, and logistics and engineering personnel.

Accordingly, by the end of the 20th century, the CF faced an array of problems:

- It was structurally and culturally constipated. It was an institution structured and focused on industrial age warfare, but without the resources to sustain it. The military leadership would not entertain the idea of a new operating model and the government was unprepared to fund the existing one.

- It had become a hollow force with declining military effectiveness, after years of economies driven by a "shaving the ice cube" philosophy.

- It faced a high, indeed unsustainable, operational tempo exacerbated by the reduction in personnel capacity.

- It held to a presumption of professionalism and a belief that specific failings were aberrations, despite evidence that it was not living up to its core military values.

- It was experiencing declining institutional cohesion due to the magnitude of changes implemented without an overarching strategy for reform.

- It faced poor and declining morale as a result of institutional failures and the lack of a clear, positive vision for the future.

It would be uncharitable or worse to the CF leadership to suggest that these problems were not recognized or that the solutions were simple. The reality was that the institution was facing such a magnitude of change that perhaps the best the leaders could do was to keep the fires under control. There were attempts to chart a more sustainable course forward. Most significant amongst these was the development of a new strategic framework, *Shaping the Future of the Canadian Forces: A Strategy for 2020* or "*Strategy 2020*", that would guide efforts to shape a new and sustainable CF.[13] Regrettably, such work lacked a coherent and compelling vision for the future. Critically, it postulated the continuation of an industrial age model and doctrine for the CF that lacked credibility with the government and virtually guaranteed no appreciable resource improvements.

In the absence of an overarching CF strategy, the various elements of the force – the navy, army and air force environments – adopted a variety of strategies and approaches to manage the, at times, impossible situation. Of the three environments, the navy appears to have best weathered the storm through this period. This can be attributed, in part, to the introduction of the Halifax class frigates and the Maritime Coastal Defence Vessels (MCDV) in the early 1990s that served as catalysts for a reform of the regular and reserve elements of the navy. The air force had to deal with significant challenges during this period as it was faced with the largest personnel reductions and a major decline in the number of its aircraft fleets. Its focus, understandably, was on the preservation of capability as it restructured to absorb the losses. However, challenged as it was with institutional failure and a continuing high tempo of operations, the army faced the most comprehensive challenge and, arguably, became the leader in terms of self-reflection and change. Starting in the late 1990s, it implemented a succession of pragmatic initiatives to improve the way it trained, generated force, and managed its resources, all with the objective of optimizing its limited capabilities. This effort reached its zenith with the development and implementation of the army strategy, starting in 2000.

While the focus of the reforms of the 1990s was very much on issues of leadership and management of the CF, there were many other lessons to be drawn from this period. Perhaps, most important were those dealing with the changing conduct of operations and the new demands for operational forces driven by this dynamic. These were principally addressed by the environmental chiefs, given their responsibility for operational doctrine and force generation. In many ways, the environments had the lion's share of the work to do in terms of adapting their organizations to the Government and CF-directed changes. Indeed, by the turn of the millennium, they were still far from having institutionalized the required reforms throughout the structure and still needed to regain balance. Change that was enacted was on an environment by environment basis, and little if any change of the integrated force was attempted.

A NEW KIND OF THREAT

On 11 September 2001 (9/11), a terrorist attack on the World Trade Towers in New York and the Pentagon in Washington set in motion a fundamental change in the way that North Americans, especially Americans, perceived their security. Never again would the continent be considered a secure haven. Thus began what some have called the Global War on Terrorism (GWOT). As early as late 2001, United Stated (US) forces were deployed in Afghanistan in a counter-terrorism campaign against Al-Qaeda. As part of Operation APOLLO, Canada contributed naval, air and ground forces to this international effort, initially under the US-led Operation ENDURING FREEDOM (OEF) and subsequently as part of the NATO-led International Security Assistance Force (ISAF). Canada was to play a major role as the mission in Afghanistan evolved.

On 20 March 2003, a US-led coalition attacked Iraq, under Operation IRAQI FREEDOM (OIF), in what has been called the Second Gulf War. While Canada did not contribute troops directly to this operation, it continued to support coalition efforts in the region under OEF, principally with naval assets. This conflict saw a very rapid advance through Iraq and a speedy capture of Baghdad, only to face a protracted counter-insurgency campaign.

Together, these two operations provided a sense of the changing nature of military operations. Apart from the initial operations in Iraq, which were based on classic industrial age mechanized tactics, these operations were decidedly asymmetrical. That is to say, conflict was between high-tech 21st century conventional forces and agrarian age tribal warriors. The result was at times a unique, even bizarre, combination of capabilities, perhaps best represented by the picture of the US Special Forces soldier on horseback in Afghanistan, directing the effects on the ground of strategic bombers. But such examples belie the serious limits that conventional military capabilities faced in this new environment. As British General Sir Rupert Smith has articulated, in "war amongst the people" the utility of force is limited.[14]

As history has proven, such a seismic shift as this new kind of threat, 9/11, this "war amongst the people", rarely occurs when expected or when an organization is prepared for it. Such was the case here. The CF, in particular the environments, was still adapting to a wide variety of policy, structural and resource changes, and was far from stable as an institution, when the real "new world order" broke onto the scene.

SUMMARY

While the CF had been shaped by the Cold War, 15 years of post-Cold War operations and events unquestionably set the stage for the real transformation that was to come. Many key reforms shaped the values, leadership, and personnel management philosophy of the CF, and the experience gained by each of the environments over a decade of demand-ing operations saw major changes in terms of how they fought. However, these changes principally were the result of tactical reactions to problems as opposed to any coherent view of where the CF needed to go. This is not to suggest that no such attempt was made, but that attempts fell short of providing a new vision essential to moving the CF forward and it clung to the view that all future operations would follow the industrial age model.

Strategic planning continued to be driven by the belief that all operations would be conventional and that the 1990s were an anomaly. In addition, despite much talk of jointness, the environments were in practice far too focused on their own worlds and more interested in combined operations with major allies. As a consequence, the CF was still thinking in terms of what environmental capabilities it could provide, rather than fully developing joint force packages. This meant, amongst other things, that deficiencies in key strategic enablers, such as command and control, airlift, surveillance and logistics essential to operating in this new environment, were allowed to persist. The reality was a continued resistance to funda-mental change and a focus strictly on maintaining "core" capabilities with ever-reducing budgets. The core of the traditional CF "industrial warfare" culture remained intact and any real transformation that was required was yet to come.

CHAPTER 2

THE NATURE OF ORGANIZATIONAL CHANGE

Essential to an informed analysis of CF Transformation is an understanding of the dynamics of any organizational change process. While the specific principles and factors will be highlighted throughout this book as part of the analysis, a general introduction to the dynamics of change and the specific subject of transformation is important to set the scene.

The subject of organizational change has become one of popular culture. Most large organizations have been through different stages of attempting to re-vitalize, streamline, right-size or re-engineer thamselves, often driven by the ideas of the latest organizational management guru. Indeed, the newsstands are full of leadership books and "how to" manuals on every imaginable aspect of organizational change. They approach the subject from a wide variety of perspectives, ranging from Margaret Wheatley's very philosophical *Leadership and the New Science*, to more practical books, such as Michael Hammer and James Champy's *Reengineering the Corporation* or the latest exposé on Total Quality Management.[15] While these books emphasize different approaches or philosophies of change, they are based largely on similar underlying factors and principles. The discussion that follows represents a compendium of the main ideas of organizational change, many drawn from the books and other sources listed as Selected Readings at the end of this book.

THE DYNAMICS OF CHANGE

The challenge facing organizational leaders contemplating change is to adjust elements of the current organization, over time, in order to realize a new system that better meets its needs. In change terms, it must focus on moving the organization from where it is currently to a new, more suitable or effective system in the future (see Figure 1).

Core to implementing such change is the need to develop a vision, a strategy and a strategic plan. The vision is a clear, simple and objective articulation of the new system to be achieved. This vision must identify a genuinely new end state that is practical and achievable. Implicit within

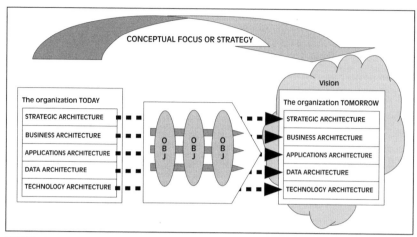

FIGURE 1: THE DYNAMICS OF ORGANIZATIONAL CHANGE[16]

this vision must be the organizational model upon which the system works, and the governance structure that it will follow. In order to achieve this vision, the leadership must develop a strategy or a conceptual focus that drives organizational change. This strategy must be the "big idea" that shapes the entire change process.

Shaped by this overarching strategy, the organization requires a strategic plan to outline the major objectives and goals to be achieved in order to realize the vision and the major approaches or strategic thrusts to be followed in pursuing it. The objectives and goals become the major phasing element of the strategy and are key to ensuring appropriate priorities are maintained, as change is implemented. The strategic thrusts ensure continuity of approach throughout the change process. While such plans may be written in great detail, their essential criterion is to provide a coherent framework to guide the implementation of change.

THE ELEMENTS OF THE ORGANIZATION

When considering organizational change, it must be understood that changes in any system need to be addressed at a number of levels. For example, introducing new technology may provide the capacity for increased effectiveness, but if the procedures and organizational cultures do not facilitate such change, no improvement will be achieved. Change initiatives must be implemented according to a framework that ensures the maintenance of a coherent and effective organization.

This framework is commonly referred to as an Enterprise Architecture, which is a model representative of the various elements of an organization and will normally depict the organization both as it is today and as it is envisioned for the future (see Figure 2).

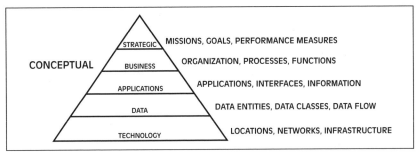

FIGURE 2: CONCEPTUAL MODEL OF AN ENTERPRISE ARCHITECTURE[17]

A more illustrative way of considering these elements is shown at Figure 3.

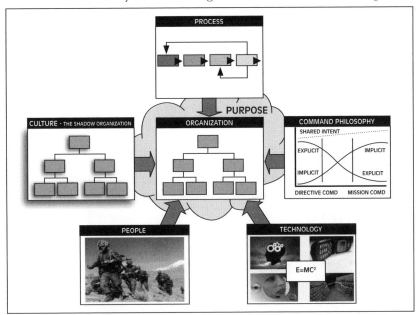

FIGURE 3: ORGANIZATIONAL ELEMENTS

Here, one must consider that any change will impact on all of these elements, albeit to varying degrees and at different rates. Thus, the challenge is to undertake change in a manner that ensures organizational coherence, by taking into account the asymmetry of change within it.

- **Purpose**. All bodies exist for a purpose that directly affects their very makeup. As the role or mission changes, or in business terms as a new product or output is required, adjustments are required in the other elements of the organization.

- **Organization**. The design of the body required to achieve this role or purpose is the principal organizational element. The primary driver of this structure is the perceived optimum means of dividing work responsibilities. However, it is greatly affected by the other organizational elements, so is in many ways an outcome of those elements.

- **Process**. In organizational terms, process is how things are done. It is a term meant to explain how the various organizational parts interact to achieve the required output or mission. In general terms, the fewer steps and organizational parts required to achieve that output, the more efficient the organization.

- **Command Philosophy.** All organizations are shaped by their command or management philosophy. In general terms, the more tactical and controlling in its philosophy, the more centralized its structure.

- **Technology**. The level of technology employed within an organization directly impacts the size and hierarchy of an organization. In principle, for a given output, increased use of technology should result in fewer people and therefore less structure in achieving it, albeit with greater support costs.

- **People**. In general, the more capable the people in an organization, the fewer people are required to achieve the task. Thus, the quality and quantity of people available for an organization will directly impact its size and structure. This quality also significantly impacts the limits of the organization, the technology used, the doctrine followed, or the command philosophy adopted.

- **Culture**. Organizational culture can be considered the personality of the organization, made up of the values, beliefs and behaviours of the organization's members. It is, in short, "how we do things" and develops as a consequence of the other organizational elements.

Healthy organizations are those in which all elements of the organization are in balance and harmony. Each is matched to the other, ensuring the optimum output. When change is induced in the system, by design or by accident, it creates an imbalance which must then be compensated for by adjustments elsewhere in the system. As an example, the introduction into the navy of the Halifax class frigates in the early 1990s required changes to many elements of the organization. The modern technology precipitated a shift in command philosophy that in turn changed the organization of the ship's crew. This demanded changes to selection and training of personnel that in turn required the development of a managed readiness system. As a consequence of these changes, the culture of the Navy over time also changed and, while many aspects of the naval culture past and present would be similar, the evolution was not insignificant.

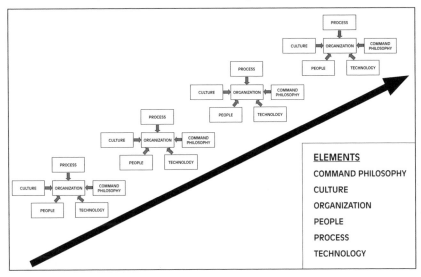

FIGURE 4: THE PROGRESSION OF CHANGE[18]

Maintaining a healthy balance of organizational elements during a period of change is difficult due to the fact that reform cannot be achieved at a uniform pace across all elements. This is in part because the organization will not have the capacity to undertake change everywhere at the same time, and in part because change takes longer to culminate in certain elements. The resulting progression of change must be carefully charted to ensure the maintenance of organizational balance over time. Figure 4 provides a depiction of this progression.

TRANSFORMATION AND CULTURE

Organizational change, either planned or unplanned, can come in many forms, generally identified by the principal change initiative.[19] Modernization, based on the procurement of new equipment and technology, undoubtedly creates a new level of capability and may induce major change in the other aspects of the institution. Restructuring the organization to improve efficiency and/or effectiveness is a common form of change. Similarly focused, process re-engineering takes a holistic view to streamline the processes of an organization. But while any of these can lead to transformation, none by itself is transformative.

Transformation is really the holistic change that results in a fundamental shift in either what an organization does or the way in which it does it. Central to this paradigm change is the development of a new or adapted organizational culture. Without a changed culture, one cannot say that a transformation has occurred.

In his book, *Hope is Not a Method*, U.S. Army General Gordon R. Sullivan highlighted what he termed a common myth that, "in the military, getting results is as easy as giving orders".[20] As he stated, the reality is that in any organization, particularly those with strong organizational culture, resistance to change can be fierce. Introducing new equipment and technology is relatively easy; re-structuring headquarters or formations is not difficult; however the closer change gets to affecting the underlying culture, the greater the difficulty becomes. Organizational culture can be defined as:

A pattern of shared basic assumptions that a group learns as it solves its problems. These solutions are successful enough to be considered valid and, therefore, should be taught to new members of the organization as the correct way to perceive, think, and feel in relation to those problems.[21]

This is particularly true with strong cultures, such as the military, where doctrine and training inculcate members with values of loyalty to their comrades and their unit and a strong sense of tradition. As a consequence, any attempt to change the organization or the way it operates is perceived as being in direct conflict with the underlying values of the culture. The result is often resistance to that change in an attempt to preserve what is seen as a valued organization or "the right way" to do things. The greater the degree of change, the greater the resistance from the organization. It is in this context that culture is often seen as the shadow organization, where the traditional values and doctrine are preserved beneath a superficial and ineffectual veneer of change.

Perhaps one of the most oft repeated examples of cultural resistance to change is the post-First World War approach by many armies to cling to the retention of cavalry, despite clear evidence of the superiority of the tank over the horse. This cultural resistance and inability to understand the changing environment is common in all organizations with strong cultures. As stated in General Sullivan's myth, change cannot be simply imposed on an organization by giving orders. Such approaches will simply be met by more resistance. It is therefore vital that change initiatives take a strategic approach that takes this resistance into account and builds, over time, the foundation of a new culture.

PHILOSOPHY OF CHANGE

There are many philosophies of how change is achieved within organizations, and many references exist to guide change leaders. These approaches largely follow the same principles, although the emphasis may shift depending on the organization or the philosophy espoused. While these references are primarily focused on business organizations, the principles are equally applicable to change within military structures. The CF was partial to John Kotter's "Eight-Stage Process of Creating Major Change" with the following key steps:[22]

- Establishing a sense of urgency for change by focusing on the crises, potential crises or opportunities faced;

- Creating a guiding coalition with enough power to lead the change and getting them to work together;

- Developing a vision to help direct the change effort and strategies for achieving that vision;

- Communicating the change vision regularly and effectively and modeling the behaviour expected;

- Empowering broad-based action by removing obstacles and changing structures that undermine the change vision and encouraging risk-taking and non-traditional ideas;

- Generating short-term wins to demonstrate that change is effective and recognizing and rewarding people who made the wins possible;

- Consolidating gains and producing more change by building on successes and the people who were effective in producing change; and

- Anchoring new approaches in the culture by rewarding positive behaviour, leadership and management as they relate to organizational success.

Whether these specific steps are followed, or not, the underlying principles are vital to the success of any organizational change. However, organizational change is a complex and difficult process, more dependent on sound leadership than any particular approach. As important as it is for an organization to have an understandable philosophy when implementing change, it is not a panacea. Change leaders must have a solid understanding of the underlying principles of organizational change to ensure success. But, above all else, they must be leaders.

CHAPTER 3

CANADIAN FORCES TRANSFORMATION

The focus of this study is institutional leadership and, specifically, the task of leading change. However, given that it is a study of CF Transformation, some general understanding of the events that have taken place and their sequence is essential. Further analysis can then build on a foundation of knowledge.

On assuming his responsibilities as CDS, General Hillier immediately commenced the process of institutional change. This process originally envisaged four phases of change, which in general have been followed. These were:

- **Phase 1**. (4 February – 30 June 2005) the development of a Vision.

- **Phase 2**. (1 July 2005 – mid 2007) the restructure of the CF operational command and control architecture.

- **Phase 3**. Alignment of the organizations and functions that are strategic and operational enablers to the new structure.

- **Phase 4**. Consideration of the evolution of Force Generation design and execution.

This overarching framework and broad sequence of phases was valid, particularly from a planning perspective, and the attention paid to many activities within the phases. However, while the phases are valid for planning, they were less useful as a framework for actual events that unfolded. Based on more recent analysis, it is more effective to identify the framework as consisting of the following change periods:

- Preparing for Change (2004 – 4 February 2005).

- Launching Transformation (4 February 2005 – end June 2005).

- Organizing Transformation (July 2005 – 1 February 2006).

- New Government Harmonization (The Battle of Visions) 1 February 2006 – mid 2007.

- Review of CF Transformation and Course Corrections (mid 2006 – 2008).

PREPARING FOR CHANGE (2004 – 4 FEBRUARY 2005)

General Hillier returned in 2004 from his tour in Afghanistan, as Commander of ISAF, with a strong sense that the CF needed to change. Over the following months, his ideas were to be shaped into a new vision for the CF. As the then-Chief of the Land Staff (CLS), he used his own strategic planning staff to shape his ideas, which, while not complete, had sufficient form for him to be able to articulate his strong views. Importantly, this work was informed by work done by an informal joint force development team drawn together through the winter – summer of 2004, and culminating in a brainstorming session at Merrickville. These "Merrickville Papers" resonated with General Hillier and reinforced his own ideas as to where the CF needed to go. This accomplishment was critical to capitalizing on the opportunity that fate would provide him later in the year.

Paul Martin assumed the reins as Canada's 21st Prime Minister (PM) on 12 December 2003 with, amongst other things, the intention of making Canada a greater player in the world.[23] He saw the CF playing a major role in this new government's foreign policy agenda and an obvious key to realizing this objective was Canada's CDS. As events would have it, the position of CDS was soon to become vacant. General Ray Henault, the CDS since 2001, was due to complete his term and had already been selected as the Chair of the NATO Military Committee. It is clear from Prime Minister Martin's public statements that, while he saw the need for more defence spending to meet his aims, he was not convinced that the status quo was what the country needed. It made eminent sense that he would be looking for a military commander who was willing to take a fresh look at the country's defence needs and the organization and capabilities of the CF.

General Hillier had already gained some public notoriety and, one must assume, profile within the government of the day. As the Commander of the NATO Multi-National Division in Bosnia in 2000 and the Commander of the ISAF in Kabul, Afghanistan in 2004, he had already proven himself as an experienced, effective and charismatic operational commander. However, it probably was his somewhat unconventional views as the CLS that gained the most attention. Frustrated with maintaining the army on a shoestring budget, he expressed the view in a letter to the CDS that, given the continuing effect of a lack of resources, perhaps trying to maintain three combat capable environments for Canada was not the best strategy for the country, and that a more focused approach might achieve better value. In this regard, he suggested, much to the displeasure of the navy and air force, that it was the army that best achieved Canada's national objectives and it should be the army that is built up. The letter's intent was to generate a much needed debate on the best kind of military for Canada. However, this internal document was leaked to the media, causing a flurry of commentary before fading from the national scene. Not surprisingly, it would continue to haunt General Hillier within the CF.[24]

In light of the PM's objectives, the views expressed by General Hillier can have been seen only as positive by the new Liberal government. At the very least, this was a man for whom the status quo was not a given. It was not a surprise, then, that General Hillier, as the youngest and most junior three-star (Lieutenant-General) in the CF, found himself on the short list of candidates for the position of CDS. Prior to Christmas 2004, he spent several hours with the PM discussing his views and vision for the CF. This interview was successful, for he quickly became the government's choice for CDS.

Given the speed with which the change of command was to occur, General Hillier immediately started to prepare for his assumption of command. Relying on select members of the staff, he conducted a mission analysis and started the work to determine how to articulate his intent and concept of operations for changing the CF. One of the key issues with which he had to deal, even before assuming command, was the matter of the evolving defence policy. The development of a new defence policy had been underway since early 2004, as part of Prime Minister Martin's *International Policy Review*. However, it had been plagued with a lack of direction and a clear resource strategy to guide a new approach.

The government's objective was clearly the development of policy that would see Canada playing a bigger role on the world stage, with a military that would be a key enabler in achieving that objective.[25] However, no such vision emerged. As evidence of the degree of frustration over a lack of progress, in late 2004, Prime Minister Martin asked Jennifer Welsh, an upcoming Canadian scholar and professor of international relations at Oxford University, to inject the policy with a new vision for the country, a vision that he felt was lacking in previous drafts prepared by the Department of Foreign Affairs. Meanwhile, having been told that no more money would be available for defence, DND took a "design to cost" approach in developing policy options. With a lack of clarity on the intent and the expectation that the department would have to live within its means, it is no wonder there was no innovation on the way ahead for the CF.

Faced with this situation, CDS-to-be LGen Hillier inserted himself into the policy development process and worked with his small policy team and some key military strategic planners to reshape the Defence Policy Statement (DPS) that had been drafted. This undertaking permitted him to further develop his vision for the CF and the development of the political themes that would underpin the future CF. In the final analysis, much of the previous policy development was sound and therefore remained. However, General Hillier's involvement brought focus to the effort and gave the government the kind of military it was seeking. He provided the "sizzle" to the previously bland steak.

While resources were, and would continue to be, an issue with respect to moving the CF forward, General Hillier was clear, as was the Minister of National Defence (MND), that, under the right circumstances, more money for defence would be available. General Hillier's challenge was to create those circumstances.

LAUNCHING TRANSFORMATION (4 FEBRUARY – END JUNE 2005)

General Hillier assumed command of the CF on 4 February 2005 and almost immediately started the planning for and "marketing" of CF Transformation. While his overall sense of where the CF needed to go was clear, there were many issues that needed to be considered, and a large amount of planning was necessary to chart a coherent approach forward. As a means of analyzing the different pieces of the problem and to develop a strategy and plan, he decided to form four CDS Action Teams (CAT). These teams started to assemble within a week of the change of command and were to focus on command and control (CAT 1), force development and generation (CAT 2), operational capabilities (CAT 3), and institutional alignment (CAT 4).

Within two weeks of assuming command of the CF, the CDS held his first General and Flag Officer (G/FO) Seminar. This was an opportunity for General Hillier to explain his vision to his generals, admirals and commodores, and to provide a sense of the magnitude of change that he foresaw. He was labouring under some restrictions, as the government's DPS had not yet been released; hence, he was limited in how much he could share with his subordinates at that stage. However, his message was one of hope and opportunity, a message that was very well received by those assembled.

The work of the CATs commenced in earnest at this mid-February G/FO Seminar, followed by a planning session at the Conference Centre in Strathmere, which focused on completion of a mission analysis and the development of work plans for the teams. The teams worked largely independently but with regular interaction with the CDS who provided guidance on an as-required basis throughout the planning period. This resulted in a degree of divergence amongst the CATs as each took a different approach to the problem. The result was less than coherent. An important and timely defence budget (presented in Parliament 23 February, and subsequently passed 28 June) gave General Hillier's transformation a much needed boost, and credibility.

In March, the CDS conducted his first Armed Forces Council (AFC) session, at which time he took his principal subordinates into his confidence on what he saw for CF Transformation. This was the first occasion where the Environmental Chiefs of Staff in particular had the opportunity to gauge the potential magnitude of the change that would be forthcoming. It was also at that meeting that the first real sense of discomfort among the senior leadership with the implications of transformation became apparent to the CDS.

At the end of June, the CDS held his second G/FO Seminar, focused solely on CF Transformation, with the CATs reporting on their work since early March. These CAT presentations were not scripted and, essentially, it was the first time the CDS had seen the specific recommendations. The differences in approach of the respective teams quickly became evident. But, more importantly, the potential magnitude of change became clear, as well as the fact that there was a significant difference of view and concern over the organizational changes being considered. The "push back" that the CDS received from his subordinates was clear, unmistakable, and a sharp contrast to the positive reception at the previous February G/FO Seminar. It was a strong indication that the transformation road would not be as smooth as envisaged.

While much planning remained to be done, it was decided that implementation of some aspects of transformation should commence as soon as possible and that a different structure would be required to achieve that. Accordingly, the CATs were disbanded following the delivery of their final reports in summer 2005 and a new CF Transformation Team (CFTT) was created to oversee and manage transformation on behalf of the CDS.

ORGANIZING TRANSFORMATION (JULY 2005 – 1 FEBRUARY 2006)

The decision to form the CFTT had been made in April 2005 and then-Major-General (MGen), now General, Walter Natynczyk was appointed Chief of Transformation (CT) in early June. The mission assigned to the CT was to:

> implement CF Transformation ... synchronized with the [Director General of Strategic Planning] DGSP, to coordinate departmental transformation activities, execute approved measures and analyze more complex issues to enable timely decisions in order to attain irreversible transformational momentum.

Based on this mission, MGen Natynczyk was assigned the following tasks by the CDS:[26]

• With Director General Strategic Planning, develop a CF Trans-formation Campaign Plan consistent with the DPS and [CDS] intent;

- Develop the Strategic Joint Staff (SJS) concept and organization to include a Concept of Operations (COO) and implementation plan;

- Develop a support concept to meet the operational requirements of Canada Command, Canadian Expeditionary Forces Command, Special Operations Group and SJS with a view to standing up a national support capability;

- Coordinate, and monitor CF Transformation initiatives;

- Facilitate, support and enable implementation of the CF Transformation;

- Develop an Integrated Managed Readiness System (IMRS);

- In consultation with the force generators, develop a force generation concept to meet the requirements of the new operational formations and current force generators; and

- With Assistant Deputy Minister (ADM) Public Affairs (PA), develop a CF Transformation communication plan.

MGen Natynczyk started building his team in June but it took most of the summer to assemble it. The final establishment of the CFTT was approximately 45 personnel, but that was never achieved. Personnel shortfalls and replacement of members were to be constant frustrations. The team was structured with a Chief of Staff (COS) with the rank of brigadier-general, four directorates each under a colonel/captain (Navy), and a number of specialist staff advisers. The four directorates included Transformation Planning that coordinated the internal activities of the CFTT, Strategic Alignment that developed options for the continued transformation of the CF Command and Control (C2) structure, Transformation Coordination that was to oversee, coordinate and monitor transformation initiatives, and Transformation Analysis that undertook limited analysis in order to provide a strategic perspective of the transformation process.

With the stand-up of CFTT, the conceptual stage of the transformation effort waned, giving way to a more concerted focus on implementation planning. With the initial members of his small team, MGen Natynczyk undertook his mission analysis and started the planning of the team's activities. By this stage, the CDS had determined that the top change priority had to be the transformation of the C2 structure of the CF and the development of sustainable integrated forces. This was to be the principal focus of the CFTT's efforts. But the determination of the future CF C2 structure required the team to do far more than facilitate the stand up of the Operations Commands. It had to take the work of the CATs, conduct its own analysis and make recommendations to shape DND and the CF. This meant shaping the strategic, national and departmental staff, reviewing Terms of Reference (ToRs), authorities, responsibilities and accountabilities, determining Force Generation options, and developing an IMRS. But, the team had to do far more than just provide the intellectual drive and future planning; it had to manage the programme as well. This meant guiding all parts of the CF through the development and promulgation of CDS Planning Guidance, maintaining situational awareness on CF Transformation, and overseeing, coordinating and monitoring transformation activities. This was a substantial and onerous task for a relatively small and centralized team.

In considering his criteria for success, the CT realized that he needed to ensure a unity of effort and to achieve effective synchronization on all transformation activities. This meant a broad engagement across the department, working to achieve a shared understanding of all transformation endeavours. He determined that he needed a strong governance structure.

Shaping the CFTT into an effective organization took considerable effort and required the development of this governance structure to ensure proper coordination. This saw the creation of two committees. The Transformation Steering Group (TSG) was designed to provide the CT with a venue for senior leadership advice, guidance and deliberation on the broader aspects of defence transformation. It was chaired by the CT and included the principal subordinates from across DND/CF. The Transformation Staff Action Team (TSAT), chaired by COS CFTT, provided a forum to assist the CT to oversee and coordinate the implementation of transformation initiatives and activities that had been approved by the CDS.

CF Command and Control. Flowing from the CAT 1 analysis on command and control, the CDS had already decided that the creation of an operational level of command external to NDHQ was an essential element of CF Transformation. This required not only the creation of new headquarters, but the complete realignment of NDHQ to a strategic-level headquarters and a reframing of the DND/CF governance structure. This understandably complex task was made more challenging by two factors. The first was the decision to stand up the operational headquarters as soon as possible to help in the creation of the "irreversible momentum" that the CDS believed essential to overcome institutional inertia. This sense of urgency meant that, while sound analysis had to be conducted to guide decision-making, risk would have to be taken and, in some cases, not all of the desirable preconditions for change could be created. The second was the reality that the full scope of the command and control change was not yet clear and there was no agreed upon or approved organization model to guide implementation. Indeed, some key decisions, such as who would be responsible for Force Generation in the CF, had yet to be made, and there was both disagreement and uncertainty as to which way this pivotal decision would go. However, such complexity is an inevitable part of change in large organizations, and the CFTT attacked the command and control challenge with vigour.

The top priority, and the core of CF Transformation, was the organization and stand up of the four operational Commands: Canada Command, Canadian Expeditionary Forces Command, Canadian Special Operations Forces Command, and Canadian Operational Support Command and the forming of the Strategic Joint Staff. This was assigned to the respective operational commanders who, in some cases, were already in place and well ahead of the CT. These commands were declared operational on 1 February 2006.

Canada Command (Canada COM). The creation of Canada COM was announced on 28 June 2005 and a designated three-star commander was appointed and provided with an initial joint planning staff of approximately 60.[27] Its initial task was to develop the final operating concept and master implementation plan, with the intention of being operationally ready as early as spring 2006. It was envisaged as one of the cornerstones of CF Transformation, responsible for the conduct of all domestic operations – routine and contingency – and would be the national operational authority for the defence of Canada and North America. Canada COM was to have its headquarters located in the National Capital Region, but separate from NDHQ, and command six joint regional headquarters – Northern, Pacific, Prairie, Central, East, and Atlantic. Its Canadian commitments and obligations were to be consistent with the NORAD agreements. Canada COM stood up officially on 1 February 2006.

Joint Task Force Atlantic (JTFA). The date of 1 July 2005 also marked the standup of Joint Task Force Atlantic, the first of six regional joint commands responsible for conducting domestic operations under Canada COM. The co-location of maritime, land and air headquarters, formations and units in and around Halifax made the Atlantic region a natural location to begin the transition to a regional joint command structure and allowed the CDS to accelerate his plans for improving integration and developing a new CF culture.

Canadian Expeditionary Forces Command (CEFCOM). In early September 2005, a planning cadre met to address the issue of CEFCOM being established, with a designated three-star commander. This unified command was to be responsible for the planning, and conduct of all CF international operations, with the exception of operations conducted solely by Canadian Special Operations Forces Command. It was to assume command of the Standing Contingency Task Force (SCTF), a high-readiness task force comprised of maritime, land, and air elements organized under a single integrated command structure; any Mission-Specific Task Forces (MSTF), task-tailored to meet mission-specific requirements, that may be deployed; and the Disaster Assistance Response Team (DART) to provide, as required, humanitarian support and disaster relief to overseas missions. CEFCOM was stood up with the other commands on 1 February 2006.

Canadian Special Operations Forces Command (CANSOFCOM). A SOG was created in September 2005 with a colonel as its commander. It later was renamed Canadian Special Operations Forces Command

and was stood up officially on February 1, 2006. It was responsible to provide the CDS and operational commanders with agile, high-readiness Special Operations Forces (SOF) capable of conducting special operations across the spectrum of conflict at home and abroad. CANSOFCOM was composed of Joint Task Force 2 (JTF2), the CF special operations and counter-terrorism unit; the Joint Nuclear, Biological and Chemical Defence Company, the Canadian Special Operations Regiment; and 427 Special Operations Aviation Squadron.

Canadian Operational Support Command (CANOSCOM). Canadian Operational Support Command was established under a two-star commander on 1 February 2006. It is responsible for planning and executing the delivery of national-level operational support for theatre activation, sustainment and termination of all CF domestic, continental and international operations. It is organized with a full range of combat support and combat environment support functions, including military engineering, health services, military police, logistics, land equipment maintenance, personnel support, resource management, and communications and information systems .

Deputy Chief of the Defence Staff (DCDS) Realignment. The magnitude of the task of creating four new operational commands was considerable. Each of the four commands had to assemble the essential personnel and organize their respective headquarters. At the same time, the DCDS had to manage the disassembly of the DCDS group and the handover of functions, responsibilities and personnel to the respective commands, all the while maintaining command and control of current and future operations until the commands were operational. The DCDS group also had to reshape part of its capability into the Strategic Joint Staff. The DCDS approached this realignment along three lines of activity. His top priority was the maintenance of effective command over operations, ensuring without interruption the direction, coordination and support to CF missions. The second priority was a focus on transformation, in particular the implementation and/or facilitation of the implementation of command and control structural changes. These were related primarily to the establishment of CEFCOM, the SJS, the SCTF, the SOG, and the

Joint Task Force North (JTF North), while divesting himself of his relative responsibilities, including domestic/continental operations responsibilities to Canada COM, which already had been stood up, when they were declared ready to assume command. Finally, the DCDS' third priority focused on the realignment of remaining capabilities, in particular the Chief of Defence Intelligence (CDI) and his critical force-development programs, as well as the restructuring of management support to meet the requirements of all elements of the transitioning structure.

In accordance with the new Conservative government's agreement to proceed with the Liberal government's plan for the command and control transformation of the CF, on 1 February 2006, the new operational commands (Canada COM, CEFCOM, CANSOFCOM, and CANOSCOM) assumed command of and responsibility for all operations, while the DCDS Group was officially dissolved on the same date.

Strategic Joint Staff (SJS). With the decision to establish the operational commands, it was decided that a small staff would remain in NDHQ to focus on strategic issues, with the mandate to:

> provide the CDS with the organic staff capability he requires to execute his two primary responsibilities; namely, the provision of military advice to the Government of Canada and the strategic command and control of CF operations.[28]

This organization was created primarily out of the DCDS Group following the stand-up of the operational commands on 1 February 2006. However, it took until the summer of 2006 before the SJS was effective in fulfilling its functions for the CDS.

NEW GOVERNMENT HARMONIZATION (THE BATTLE OF VISIONS) 1 FEBRUARY 2006 – MID 2007

With the election of a new government on 23 January 2006 and the swearing in of a new Cabinet on 6 February, CF efforts to transform hit some rough water. The defence objectives of the Conservative government were, and had to be seen as, different from the previous Liberal government.

In addition, there was a new MND, the Honourable Gordon O'Connor, with a high level of experience within DND and strong views as to what needed to be done to "fix" the CF. The new government's objectives for defence were to some degree at variance with General Hillier's vision and, unquestionably, the total level of ambition (O'Connor & Hillier) was beyond the resources or the capacity of the CF. Thus began what can only be termed a battle of visions.

Importantly, this period coincided with a shift of CF operational focus in Afghanistan to Kandahar and an increase in intensity of operations that, sadly, included Canadian casualties.

With the arrival of a new government, DND turned its attention to adjusting its approach and priorities to meet a new set of objectives and expectations. This was not an unusual or particularly worrisome task as the change of Ministers and governments is a well-exercised dynamic. However, as events were to prove, this was no ordinary transition.

As early as the fall of 2005, it had become clear that the overall level of ambition of the DND/CF was too great for the institution to handle. The department was already facing a significant challenge, given the very high tempo of operations, efforts to transform the CF, increased recruitment and training driven by the need to regenerate the forces, and ongoing efforts to re-equip the CF. However, three aspects of the Conservative defence platform added significantly to this load: a greater emphasis on capability dedicated to domestic defence and security, in particular in the north, under the Canada First strategy; a commitment to considerably expand the CF; and a desire to implement major new capital projects. These new demands would not have been an issue had the CF the capacity to meet all of these needs, but that was not the reality. As a consequence, there unfolded a significant debate on the priorities or the vision for the CF.

Resourcing of defence in Canada has been and perhaps always will be a major challenge. However, in 2006, the institution was only just coming out of a long period of drought or, as some have called it, a "decade of darkness", created in large measure by the debt-fighting financial strategies of the 1990s.[29,30] Faced with rust-out of the equipment fleets and a growing demographic crisis as the CF aged, the military leadership needed to invest every penny it could in equipment and personnel program. At the same time, an increasing operational tempo was demanding more money to sustain the weapons and people that were already in service. This situation did not preclude new initiatives by the government, but it did mean a significant re-prioritization of the existing program.

Dollars, however, were not the only concern, for availability of experienced personnel was rapidly becoming the dominant factor on the critical path to undertaking any new activities. All of the CF's major activities (training, equipment acquisition, transforming the command and control structure, and conducting of operations) required good quality, experienced officers and non-commissioned members (NCM). These critical leaders and managers were already experiencing stress problems, given the demands on them, so doing more was not an option. Someone had to set new priorities.

Faced with this situation, the Deputy Minister (DM) of National Defence and CDS formed a staff working group to develop options for aligning the CF vision and strategy with the new government's stated intent and priorities within the existing resource framework. This work saw the development of numerous options and the discussion, indeed the negotiation, of priorities and activities to be undertaken with the Minister. This dynamic was not an easy one and created real pressures at the top. Ultimately, changes to planned activities were made and progress was achieved. Perhaps most notable in this regard was the announcement in June 2006 of five major capital projects (Joint Support Ships, Strategic Airlift, Tactical Airlift, Medium Lift Helicopters, and Medium Lift Trucks). However, it also saw ministerial decisions that created difficulty for the CDS, especially on the transformation front. Here, the suspension of the SCTF, a centrepiece of General Hillier's vision, was a serious blow.

Despite the difficulties from these ministerial decisions, compromise between the new government and the CF was achieved with respect to both vision and strategy. Ultimately, a plan was taken to government. However, given the demands of defence and other priorities, the CF strategy was held in abeyance. When Minister O'Connor was reassigned as part of the cabinet shuffle in summer 2007, while certain priorities and activities had been agreed upon, the defence strategy had advanced no further.[31]

REVIEW OF CF TRANSFORMATION AND COURSE CORRECTIONS (MID-2006 – 2008)

By mid-2006, with the four operational commands established, the CDS identified the need for an independent assessment of the new command structure, in order to identify and refine Phase 2 activities, and to set the stage for Phases 3 and 4 of CF Transformation. In short, he needed to take stock of the state of affairs of the CF and in particular the changes implemented as a guide to making some mid-course corrections. This was particularly so, given the momentum lost as a result of the focus on harmonizing the visions.

To achieve this, the CDS asked three retired senior officers, LGen Fred Sutherland, a former Vice Chief of the Defence Staff (VCDS), and Vice-Admiral Lynn Mason and LGen Ray Crabbe, both former DCDSs, to undertake a validation study of the transformed CF Command Structure focused on force employment. The validation team delivered its first report on 31 January 2007 and its second report on 5 September 2007.[32] In addition, during this period, the VCDS initiated a Functional Review of the operations functions and resource allocation within the operational level of command.

The reports provided the CDS an opportunity to reflect on CF Transformation and to make course corrections to ensure his overall objectives were achieved. Unquestionably, they provided the CDS with a good sense of the state of CF Transformation and some very clear ideas as to how he needed to shape the process going forward. However, while the reports did result in adjustments to the transformation plans, the degree to which the recommendations were embraced or implemented is less clear.

Perhaps, the most significant of the recommendations made to the CDS was that he, as the face of CF Transformation, personally re-engage in the process and champion the effort, particularly the cultural transformation he envisaged for the CF. This, along with the insight the reports provided into the degree of unity, or lack thereof, amongst the CF leadership, galvanized the CDS into action. Accordingly, the CDS used this as the focus for his May 2007 G/FO Seminar with a clear intent to recalibrate the CF Transformation effort and to ensure that his leadership team was well aligned to re-energize the initiative.

Notwithstanding the CDS' intent on coming out of the G/FO Seminar with a much enhanced unity and alignment of his leadership team, there appears to have been no coherent refocusing of Transformation. The CDS did, as promised, publish a revised vision and clarified his intent with respect to his Transformation principles in his SITREP # 5. However, the overall CF Transformation entered a consolidation phase that, for the most part, lasted to the end of General Hillier's tenure in mid-2008. This is not to suggest that the thinking on the subject has stopped. Indeed, the very phasing of Transformation has moved beyond the original four phases. These never were intended to be sequential and, in practice, the CF found itself in early 2008 at a point where phases 2, 3 and 4 were all at some stage of implementation. Perhaps, a more effective portrayal of the CF Transformation plan was the use of the "missile" metaphor that the CDS

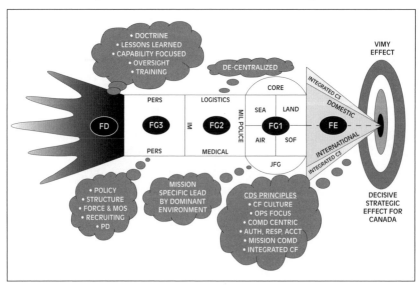

FIGURE 5: THE CDS' TRANSFORMATION MISSILE

had developed during 2007 to explain the phases. This reflects the overall design of the CF as a rocket or missile with each stage as the respective process elements of the organization. Using this model, change was being implemented at all stages commencing at the tip with Force Employment (FE) and progressing in turn through the various stages of Force Generation (FG) to the fuel of Force Development (FD) (Figure 5).[33]

SUMMARY

This work is a snapshot of the first two years of CF Transformation. It is not intended to address the current state and activities. Indeed, the majority of the research on the project was completed by September 2007. However, given that the year 2008 has seen a period of consolidation of the CF Transformation, and that the conclusions, assessment of lessons learned, and identification of future challenges, as relevant as of 2008, are being addressed in this book, this publication essentially reflects a three-year history, 2005-2008, of CF Transformation. What follows during and after 2009 might very well deserve yet another book.

CHAPTER 4

VISION – THE CRITICAL INGREDIENT

Every new organizational direction starts with a fresh idea; a general sense of a requirement for a new order of things. This kernel of thought may emerge from one mind or a variety of minds almost simultaneously. In order to move the organization forward, this idea must find expression as an understandable description of the objective to be achieved. This vision of the organization's future provides the focus for change.

A vision for the future is not just some vague idea of where the organization should go but is the result of much serious thought and often years of experience within the organization. A change leader must see the world as it is and will be, and see the organization's evolving place in that world and how it must change to remain relevant, all of this in sufficient detail to guide the organization forward. Most importantly, he must have a strong conviction that his vision is correct.

To be credible and to get people to buy in, the vision needs to be inspiring, inclusive and eventually achievable. The vision must enthrall people and make the future attractive. Implicit in this, it must be easily understood, necessitating a simple depiction of often complex concepts. The essence of the "big idea", which is the new organization's focus, must shine through that simplicity. In order to "buy in", all must be able to see themselves or their organization and culture within the vision. This will be a challenge, as major change will mean that much of the current culture must disappear and this will naturally alienate many people. The change leader must find a way, explicitly or implicitly, to show where all can have a place in his new idea. Finally, the vision must be one that all see as possible – one that can be realized. Overly ambitious or ill-considered ideas, which all perceive as having little chance of success, will only spark cynicism. Properly structured and communicated, a vision will not only launch fundamental change, motivating all to follow the change leader, but it will sustain that change through the, at times, dark and difficult days of implementation.

CHAPTER 4

THE ORIGIN OF THE IDEA

As with many ideas, General Hillier's sense of the problems facing the CF, and the essence of the change that he saw as necessary, developed over time and there is no doubt that his experience was fundamental to shaping his emerging vision. General Hillier spent much of his time as a field commander. As the Commander of 2 Canadian Mechanized Brigade Group, he participated in domestic operations focused on the 1997 Red River Floods and the 1998 Ice Storm. Subsequently, he completed a tour as Deputy Commander of III (US) Corps in Fort Hood, Texas, where he had the opportunity to experience the culture and approaches of a different and much larger military. He also served under NATO command as the Commander of Multinational Division Southwest (MND SW) in Bosnia. But, perhaps most influential was his tenure as Commander ISAF in Kabul, Afghanistan, where he had ample opportunity to experience, first hand, the type of evolving asymmetric conflict found around the world, to develop an intimate understanding of the CF's ability to meet the emerging demands of such conflicts, and to shape his ideas of how the CF should evolve.

On his return to Canada, as CLS, he worked with his key strategic planning staff to further develop his ideas. This work was importantly influenced by work done by an informal joint force development team that had started back in 2002 when DND/CF was trying to create a defence program that was both relevant to government needs and affordable in the projected fiscal framework. Much of this work was drawn together through the winter, spring and summer of 2004, culminating in a brainstorming session at Merrickville. The key idea that emerged from Merrickville was that of a high readiness expeditionary task force. These "Merrickville Papers" resonated with General Hillier and reinforced his own ideas as to where the CF needed to go. Once advised that he would be appointed CDS, the effort to define his vision accelerated.

Central to General Hillier's sense of the need for change in the CF was his concern over the institution's operational effectiveness. While the CF had generally performed well in a variety of missions and environments, General Hillier saw the Canadian contribution as increasingly rudimentary, unresponsive to mission needs, and providing Canada with a poor return on investment. This situation was a consequence of the CF's traditional "industrial warfare" force structure and operational doctrine, a non-responsive and bureaucratic approach to C2, and an environment oriented culture, all of which he saw as impeding the effectiveness and limiting the ability of the CF to meet the missions to be faced in the 21st century.

The relevance of CF's force structure and operational doctrine. The CF, like most modern militaries, is structured primarily for conventional warfare. This is a consequence of Canada's historic engagement in European conflicts and its commitment to European defence through NATO. This saw Canada's navy, army and air force as miniature versions of larger militaries, structured and trained principally for combined operations under NATO command. Such an approach did not preclude undertaking other types of operations, such as peacekeeping, either independently or as part of other organizations and alliances. However, it required the CF to adapt to meet these requirements. The philosophy was one that saw the CF organized, equipped and trained for the most challenging type of conflict, "industrial age" warfare, in the expectation that it could adapt to handle any "lower order" conflict with relative ease. This approach unquestionably resulted in some aspects of the force being sub-optimal for these other types of missions. But, this was seen as an acceptable risk, compared with the alternatives.

With the end of the Cold War and the growth in new types of missions, militaries were starting to question the validity of this organizational philosophy. There was a growing sense that the likelihood of "industrial age" war was increasingly remote but that, as General Sir Rupert Smith describes it, "war amongst the people" would be the dominant type of conflict in the 21st century.[34] However, what that means in terms of specific doctrine, organization, equipment and training remains unclear. So, while there is increasing agreement that the old ways are not what is needed, there is great uncertainty as to what is needed. Consequently, the least risk was seen as retaining the old ways until new ones evolved, even though they may not be applicable and may result in scarce capability that is not useable. Of course, one of the major difficulties with this issue is the reality that, even though a new form of conflict may be emerging, it does not negate the fact that all of the weapons of warfare still existed and would be used by potential opponents. So, balancing the organization, doctrine and equipment to meet the urgent needs, while maintaining sufficient capability to respond to the less likely, but potentially more dangerous, requirements is the real dilemma facing the force developer.

As General Hillier saw it, a small military such as the CF, facing serious resource limitations, could ill afford to maintain a lot of capability that was not useful on a routine basis. In short, Canada was facing a global environment where "war amongst the people" was the greatest threat, and it needed to focus its efforts there. This did not imply the absence of a requirement to face the possibility of conventional conflict, for this risk remained, even if in isolated situations. It meant a shift in the focus from conventional/industrial warfare (with the ability to adapt to other forms of conflict) to preparation for asymmetric conflict (three-block war) with the ability to adapt to conventional/industrial warfare.[35] It meant not an exchange of one type of capability for another but rather the movement of the weight of effort more in favour of the real needs of operations in the 21st century, as well as an acceptance of risk in a different part of the response spectrum.

A bureaucratic and efficiency-oriented C2 process. While the CF approach to command and control has evolved over the years, its fundamentals remained largely the same between the mid-1970s and 2006. Strategic command is vested in the CDS but had been exercised through the DCDS who managed and coordinated all operational issues on his behalf. The DCDS would conduct all planning for potential missions, including developing commitment options for the government, supported by the environmental chiefs who would generate the forces to be deployed.

The process employed under the DCDS was effective in terms of analyzing the options available to the government and the overall risks faced by the CF, but it tended to be somewhat superficial in its assessment of the specific mission to be undertaken. This was the result of years of mission planning under UN and NATO leadership, where the overall strategy and the mission operational planning were left very much to others. Given that Canada would be contributing components or elements of the force, at times very small elements, assessment of the tactical situation on the ground and the role to be performed did not feature high in planning. The military assessment tended to focus on the CF capability to support the mission and overall risk. In turn, the political considerations for commitment tended to focus on the value of having the Canadian flag present on the mission balanced against the inherent risks. As a consequence, the "intent" of Canada's commitment, beyond participation, was often uncertain, with no clear national objective. Consequently, there was no "responsibility" for mission success so, provided the risks were acceptable, consideration of capabilities beyond the established affordability were moot. A reasonable force package that permitted Canadian participation was the objective.

Once committed by the government, the tactical forces generated would be deployed into the mission area and placed under operational command of a national contingent commander. They would in turn be assigned, normally under operational control, to the alliance/multinational commander. Thereafter, despite the national limitations (caveats) placed on this assignment, from a practical perspective, the operational planning for the mission was conducted by the multinational headquarters. The result was to leave the deployed national contingent commander, once on the ground, to try to employ the resources he had been given to achieve the objectives that his international commander set for him and to mitigate the risks faced as best he could. At NDHQ, beyond maintaining situational awareness of the mission and routine sustainment of the force, the DCDS' primary involvement in a mission once the force was deployed was to address requests for changes to national caveats. This approach led to a culture in which operational mission issues were routinely handled by the staff and, without clear intent for the deployed mission, a lack of support and responsiveness. As missions became more demanding and risks increased, this staff approach led to a heightened sense of potential for mission failure.

The command and control issues, however, were not confined to the international stage. Indeed, in some respects the situation with domestic operations was even worse. Historically, Canada's military has been run on a "force generation" philosophy. That is to say, wars were to be fought somewhere else and the primary focus of our military effort was in generating the troops to send overseas. This does not mean that the defence of Canada was not important, and forces were continually assigned to guard the maritime and air approaches. Given a long history without direct threats and over 40 years of Cold War stability, however, the philosophy was very much one of a fortress North America. Specifically, air defence was handled by NORAD while maritime defence was left primarily to the navy and, over time, the national capacity to command and control the domestic defence mission waned. Indeed, when faced with domestic operational requirements, the DCDS had to augment his small "continental" staff for the duration of the crisis. This situation was exacerbated by the fact that the C2 structure in Canada was not streamlined to support joint operations. One example highlighted in the CAT 1 study report demonstrated that in Atlantic Canada alone there were no less than 19 separate CF chains of command.[36] In a post-9/11 world, with domestic security an increasing concern, such a level of responsiveness was considered unacceptable.

Environment-oriented cultures that impede CF effectiveness. Navies, armies and air forces have different cultures, as demanded by their operational environments. While the able seaman aboard a frigate, the aviation technician on the flight line and the infantry rifleman on patrol may all be professional in their own right, the demands of their business require different approaches. However, when deployed on a common mission, facing similar threats, these environmental cultures and approaches must meet the needs of that environment. The army air defence detachment deployed aboard ship must have sufficient understanding of the operational procedures and appropriate training to act as members of the crew. In the same manner, a naval cook deployed as part of a land-based operational mission must be sufficiently prepared to be effective in that environment.

Such a philosophy was implicit in the post-unification CF but, over the years, increasing financial and operational pressures resulted in erosion of common training standards and reluctance on the part of the environments to seriously consider other environmental needs. The CF standard became *defacto* the lowest common denominator. Over time, this also saw the emergence of cultural communities, often irrespective of the uniforms they wore, with unique operational experience and little ability or interest in employment outside of that environment. The cooks aboard ship, on the flight line or in the infantry battalion, may have the same trade skills, but they often were not employable outside of their narrow operational training and experience. Importantly, over time, the willingness to accept cross employment decreased.

As the demands on the CF to support operational missions increased, there was a need to cast a wider net for personnel and, increasingly, a requirement to deploy people outside their traditional training and experience. This approach was supported by increased pre-deployment training but with ever increasing operational risks. Ultimately, given the lack of sound common training, cultural understanding became a limiting factor in joint operations. The result was a CF composed of three environments with different, often conflicting, cultures and different philosophies as to how that mission should be accomplished. At times, the environments could not even agree on the terminology to be used, in view of differing roles and missions, different doctrine and strategic perspectives.[37]

The essence of the vision. To address these concerns, General Hillier foresaw a new kind of CF and shaped his vision statement accordingly.[38] It indicated that the CF "will become more effective, relevant and responsive, and its profile and ability to provide leadership at home and abroad will be increased."[39] Specifically it stated that the Forces will become:

- More effective by better integrating maritime, land, air and special operations forces. The overall goal will be 'focused effects': the ability to deploy the right mix of forces to the right place, at the right time, producing the right result;

- More relevant, both at home and abroad. They will adapt their capabilities and force structure to deal, in particular, with threats that arise from the kind of instability that we have seen abroad, especially in failed states; and

- More responsive by enhancing their ability to act quickly in the event of crises, whether in Canada or around the world. They will arrive on the scene faster, make a rapid transition to operations once there, move more effectively within theatre, and sustain deployments, in some cases, for extended periods.

Implicit in this vision, General Hillier saw three fundamental changes to the *modus operandi* of the CF:

- **A shift of institutional focus**. General Hillier saw CF transformation as shifting the focus of the institution away from its post-Cold War mind set, placing a much higher priority on domestic and continental security, but also playing a greater role on the world stage. He saw shaping the force to deal with the growing challenge of failed and failing states, and envisaged a capability that would permit it to fight the evolving three-block war. This meant a force able to undertake a full range of military roles from humanitarian assistance and peace support operations to counter-insurgency operations, while retaining the core capabilities essential to conduct industrial age warfare.

- **A paradigm shift in command philosophy**. General Hillier also saw a paradigm shift in command philosophy. The CF would have a unified command and control structure that saw a clear command chain for operations, with the CDS at the apex. Adoption of a command-centric philosophy would reassert command to its rightful place, with an appropriate subordination of the staffs. Finally, a mission-command approach would ensure that subordinate commanders had the latitude required to fulfill their mission without constant micro-management from above. The result would be a more agile C2 structure and improved operational effectiveness of the CF.

- **An integrated CF culture**. Finally, the CDS saw the development of an integrated CF culture, a force where environmental objectives were subordinate to the greater good of the CF and the nation. He saw integrated CF effort resulting in focused and integrated effects in operations to ensure all elements of the CF were able to contribute effectively to the mission. This was envisaged to be a positive, constructive change that would see all elements of the CF as part of one team, while still respecting the uniqueness of their respective roles. This philosophy would provide the foundation for a much broader and cooperative "Team Canada" approach under the government policy of defence, diplomacy and development.

BROADER OBJECTIVES

However, also implicit in General Hillier's vision were objectives that went much further than simply changing the nature of the military institution. He envisaged a new strategic paradigm in which the military would have a more important role in helping the nation realize its strategic objectives, would truly be part of the fabric of the nation and, as a consequence, would have the support, in both moral and resource terms, of the people and government.

Creating the Vimy effect. Key to the achieving of this new vision was focusing CF effort, in all that it did, on achieving a strategic effect. This did not represent a change of structure or even operational doctrine; rather, it was a fundamental shift in thinking. The CDS entreated his officers to think strategically and to ensure that the CF contribution, wherever it was made, would have value beyond its size. General Hillier envisaged a quality force that was focused in such a way to achieve effects far greater than the relatively small contribution Canada could make on the world stage. By April 2007, he often referred to this as the "Vimy effect", in reference to the historic First World War battle where a tactical victory by the Canadian Corps was to have strategic impact, earning Canadian troops a new respect, and Canada greater autonomy as a nation and a greater voice in the world.

Connecting with Canadians. Having served through the difficult period of the 1990s, including the public vilification of the military resulting from the Somalia Inquiry, General Hiller vowed that the CF would never again find itself separated from the population from which it flowed. He, as all professional military officers are, was convinced that in order to maintain its moral authority the CF must be part of the fabric of Canadian society. The CF had to belong to the people and there had to be a bond between the forces and all Canadians. This he saw not as a political act but as one essential to maintaining the legitimacy of a military force in a democratic country. It meant being accessible to the people, communicating with Canadians and, above all else, being transparent as an institution. He knew that Canadians would not send their sons and daughters to serve if they did not trust the CF as an institution. Credibility and trust were the keys.

Improving the resource situation. Unquestionably, one of the targets of General Hillier's efforts was to improve the resource and sustainability problem of the CF. This is not unique and every CDS has had his challenges in seeking a better defence budget. Indeed every government expected to hear pleas for more money. General Hillier knew that if the CF was to remain relevant to the nation, in particular given the security challenges it was likely to face, a real change in the resource situation had to be achieved. However, he was equally sure that a status quo approach with respect to the military requirement was not acceptable, as Paul Martin had made very clear on the day he was sworn in as Prime Minister.[40]

ASSESSMENT OF THE VISION

There is no question that debate over the kind of military Canada needs to meet its defence requirements in a changing world is timely and germane. Ever since the end of the Cold War, there has been much commentary and debate, both in Canada and internationally, about the changing requirements of defence and security. Indeed, in many quarters, there has been a search for that new paradigm, that new conceptual model, that shapes military doctrine and structure to satisfy the needs of the 21st century.

As a professional soldier who had on several occasions lived that new security environment as an operational commander, General Hillier intuitively understood the nature of the changes around him. He also had a strong sense of the changes required within the CF to meet the challenges of this new environment and overcome its institutional shortcomings. That is not to say that he saw all aspects of the issue with the clarity that one would hope for, but he did so with sufficient focus to be certain of the need for change. Given that context, it should come as no surprise that the large majority of those in uniform saw his vision as the right direction for the CF. As professionals, most had long sensed that change was inevitable and many had been frustrated by the organization's rigidity.

The vision was inspirational to those serving, perhaps in large measure because it provided a positive sense of direction and hope that the long period of difficult times was coming to an end. While it did not specifically promise more resources, it made clear the CDS' expectation that they would flow. This message of optimism, delivered in a forceful and convincing manner, was exactly what the CF needed so it is no wonder that, on several occasions following his address on CF Transformation, the CDS received a standing ovation. Still, not all were convinced and some had difficulty seeing themselves in this future. The navy and the air force in particular saw this new vision, with such metaphors as the "three block war", as very much army-centric. To some degree, this criticism was valid. The vision focused on failed and failing states and, while it included the requirement to operate in the littorals and envisaged all environments playing a role, the major operations were expected to be on the land.

In fairness, the vision was a pragmatic approach to some difficult realities. It acknowledged that successive governments had shown no interest in resourcing the CF to the levels required to maintain full spectrum combat capability at home and abroad, and sought to achieve an optimal balance while preserving combat capability. There was no question that the CF required effective capabilities as part of the defence of Canada and North America, and most saw intuitively that guarding Canada's perimeter and surveilling its land mass was air and sea-power heavy. The critical question was how would Canada get best value or return on its military investment on the international stage. General Hillier's view was that it is failed and failing states where the greatest international need is, and it would be "boots on the ground" that provide Canada voice and influence around the world. This was not to suggest that the navy and air force were not included in his vision, but that their highest value contribution to the nation's international role may well be in support of land-centric missions.

Concerns were also expressed at the outset over the achievability of the vision. Clearly the plans implicit in this new approach demanded significant resources and, some asked, how these would be realized given the resource shortages the CF was already facing. Again, this was a valid concern. After all, the majority of those serving had lived through some of the leanest times and, while things were improving, there still was not a great deal of resource flexibility in the organization. Many could do the calculations and see that, given the probable costs of the CDS' plans, some of the CF's core capabilities could be in jeopardy.

Few understood that the strategy that General Hillier had adopted was focused in part on improving the resource situation. He expected that by reshaping the CF, such that it would provide greater value for the nation, the government would better resource the institution. Indeed, it is probable, given his discussions with the PM and the MND, that some level of understanding was achieved that more money would come to Defence. However, he could not say so publicly and so had difficulty in assuaging concerns over achievability. As a consequence, many took a "wait and see" attitude with respect to Transformation.

Reshaping the vision. Through a significant period of implementation and challenges of harmonizing his plans with the new government's plans and priorities, the CDS' vision survived reasonably well. Perhaps the greatest blow it received was the MND's decision not to approve work on the SCTF that had been identified by the CDS as one of the four force structure pillars of the transformed force.[41] While the specific model he had chosen could not be implemented, the underlying philosophy of an integrated operational structure and capability remained valid. In the same vein, the resource challenges that had become apparent indicated that not all of the expectations could be met. Here again, the problem was not with the vision *per se* but rather in the people's expectations of it. Even with resource challenges, the vision remained valid. These blows to the vision as stated were not insignificant, however, and were seen by some as evidence that transformation would fail.

By early 2007, with the passage of time and the effects of an evolving government policy or intent, it became clear that some elements of the vision needed to be reconsidered. Central to this perspective was the report on the "Validation of the Transformed CF Command Structure" that addressed a number of concerns over understanding and acceptance of the vision. Accordingly, the CDS focused his May 2007 G/FO Seminar on Transformation, and sought the view of his senior officers on the state of change. In this context, while many saw positives in the vision and felt progress was being made, it was clear that many still did not fully understand the intent or see themselves in it. As a result of this feedback, the CDS committed himself to developing a new vision statement that took their concerns into account.

The revised statement published in October 2007 stated that the CF was to be:

> …an effective, integrated, military force valued by allies, partners and friends that stands ready to protect Canada and Canadians and, through the conduct of its missions, gives our country the strategic impact to shape and protect Canadian interests.[42]

Whether this revised vision statement will better meet the needs of the CF and satisfy the expressed concerns, only time will tell.

SUMMARY

General Hillier envisaged a more effective, relevant and responsive CF with significant strategic value to Canada. To achieve this vision, he intended a shift away from a focus on industrial age conflict, a paradigm shift in command philosophy, and the development of an integrated CF culture. Perhaps most significant, he saw the need for the CF to become part of the fabric of Canadian society. This vision was one that was easily understood and that resonated with many, both in uniform and out. Indeed, it was just what he needed to guide his plans for Transformation. The challenges he faced were in creating the right environment in which this vision could flourish.

CHAPTER 5

CREATING THE ENVIRONMENT FOR CHANGE

When facing the potential for organizational change, rarely does the change leader encounter an environment that is fully conducive to realizing the change envisaged. No matter how strong the leader, organizational change requires support for the change leader's ideas, both internally and externally, in order to be successful. The stronger that support, the greater will be the chances of success. It therefore falls to the change leader to create the positive circumstances required, indeed to shape the environment, as a vital first step in creating the foundation for the transformation effort. The level of support that he can generate will shape the strategy that he follows, will dictate how quickly he can proceed, and may even alter the vision he will try to achieve.

The change leader must sell his idea or his vision to those most influential in its achievement. In a military context, this includes the government leadership and influential actors both within and outside the government bureaucracy. But, the focus must be on the people within the organization. The change leader must convince them not only of the need to change, but the wisdom of his vision, and must imbue them with a sense of urgency to get it done. He must develop a shared vision and in time a sense of unity within the organization, requiring him to understand the views of all stakeholders and to have a good sense of the impact change will have on them. He must also develop a change team to help him in his quest, for no change leader can do it alone. All of these circumstances require detailed attention and concerted effort.

Communicating the vision. The vision fulfills two vital functions. It is the organization's target, focusing people on where the organization must go, and guiding them on how they must adapt. But, it is also the fuel for that change, inspiring people with the new idea and energizing them to achieve it. Creating this energy requires the vision to be communicated to the people within the organization effectively, frequently and personally by the change leader. It is his vision and he must put a strong personal touch on its expression, imbuing the organization with his passion and sense of urgency. That communication should not be limited to the organization itself. The change leader must sell his idea or his vision to those most influential in its achievement. This must start with the government leadership, but often includes influential actors both within and outside the government bureaucracy. The change leader is marketing his plans to achieve both acceptance of the vision and genuine support for the change process to be undertaken. This salesmanship must be based on the change leader's change strategy and his communications strategy. These challenges are discussed in greater detail in Chapters 6 and 7.

Developing a shared vision. No matter how clear or prescient the vision, no one can effectively change an organization by force. Change must start with a general acceptance of the need for and nature of the change envisaged. This implies that the change leader must develop a shared vision, first and foremost amongst the senior leadership but over time throughout the organization.

Such a shared view can be achieved by convincing subordinates of its correctness, in short by the leader shaping his subordinates to his will. Such approaches do have their limitations. Achieving real ownership of the vision requires people to engage in the intellectual exercise of debating its purpose and substance until reaching a point when they can agree with it. This requires an open approach to debate on the subject and a degree of compromise on everyone's part. The secret for the change leader is to compromise in a manner that enhances the unity of the team without eroding the soundness of the vision. Indeed, such an inclusive approach ideally should produce a stronger, more achievable "shared" vision.

Developing the change team. Central to managing and progressing change is a core change team. This team should be composed of people equally committed to the task and possessing the leadership, skills, credibility and authority to shape the organization.[43] This team must be, in the mind of the change leader, the source of many of the good ideas and must provide much of the energy for change. The team must be an extension of the change leader.

Ideally, this core change team should be based upon the executive leadership team.[44] However, this very much depends on the tasks to be performed and the chemistry of the leadership team. The change leader may not have unanimous engagement from the executive leadership team and therefore must take steps to move the change process forward despite their views. This, of course, shapes what role members of the executive leadership team play. Some will be at the centre of the change initiative, while others may be asked to provide leadership in parts of the organization least affected by change.

Developing unity. Beyond creating a shared vision, the change leader needs to achieve, over time, a high degree of unity in the change process. It may start with a general acceptance of the vision, but must grow to the majority embracing the vision and the implied concepts of operations, and the new culture that will achieve them. This unity of thought, purpose and action must become the cement that binds the emerging organizational culture together. In short, this means creating a dynamic where many within the organization are actively advancing the change process with a clear idea of where they need to go. Building and maintaining such a level of unity is very difficult and a change leader must balance the need to engage his subordinates, to seek consensus, with his determination to achieve change.

Unity also means achieving a high degree of strategic coherence, achieved through development of a strategy and plans with defined goals and objectives that are aligned and consistent with the operational commitments and resource availability of the organization.[45] Such coherence ensures that people who had difficulties embracing the vision, in part because they did not see themselves in it, can nonetheless accept those goals as important improvements in the organization.

ASSESSMENT

The manner of communicating the vision. General Hillier was most effective in articulating his vision. Indeed, communication has been General Hillier's strength and he built upon it from the time he was appointed CDS. After years of corporate military leadership, the institution was enthralled by this natural, personable communicator. Perhaps most important was the manner in which the vision was delivered, for General Hillier's style attracted many looking for an uplifting message. He took every opportunity to speak to people, not only his internal CF audience but his external audience, in particular the people of Canada. A charismatic and populist leader, he captured the imagination of CF members, government, industry, and indeed Canadians, with his style, and he inspired them with his vision for a new CF.

Achieving a shared vision. Effectively communicating his vision did not assure the CDS of acceptance of that vision. Of all challenges that General Hillier faced, achieving a shared vision, particularly among his senior leaders, was the most difficult. Having developed his vision, he first tested it on his G/FOs at a seminar in February 2005. His vision of a revitalized CF in which the existing problems would be fixed, and the force would be modernized and made more relevant to the national needs, understandably struck a chord. He was enthusiastically embraced by his officers who left that initial session buoyed by the prospect of change. However, as so often happens, all saw in that vision what they wanted to see and few fully understood the implications of the changes proposed.

General Hillier believed that the majority of the G/FOs, especially the more junior ones, were, like him, products of a new, more operationally focused generation of corporate leaders and that they shared many common experiences. He anticipated that they would, for the most part, share his willingness to change. Following the reception at the first G/FO Seminar, he understandably was persuaded that all were on board. However, by the second seminar, held in June, many had started to voice reservations over the vision and its implications, clearly indicating that this vision was not shared by all. Indeed, it is probable that he never achieved a truly shared vision amongst his senior leadership team.

Part of the challenge he faced was due to the time he had and the manner in which he developed the vision. There is no question that General Hillier relied greatly on others to help him develop his vision, but the process was not altogether inclusive. Certainly, the insights provided by a range of force development staff and trusted agents prior to his CDS appointment were most influential in shaping his ideas. In addition, the work of the

CATs, supported by a wide variety of discussions with his senior leaders, brought clarity to a number of elements. In turn, primarily through the medium of the CDS seminars, he also engaged his G/FOs. However, time limited an initial collective visioning process and no real shared vision was embraced by the CF's senior leadership. There was acceptance of the vision and many worked to implement elements of it, but issues of inclusiveness and achievability persisted, and there remained a sense of uncertainty as to where the CF was going. Following the first validation report in January 2007, the CDS looked seriously at this issue.[46]

The concerns held by the leadership, particularly those of inclusiveness and achievability, were understandable and typical of any organization undergoing such change. To the degree that he could, General Hillier attempted to assuage those concerns. However, he faced limits in balancing the promise and the reality of his vision. The truth was that reshaping the CF could see both winners and losers, depending on the willingness of the government to increase defence funding, and/or their stomach for divesting itself of certain capabilities. With the arrival of a new government with its own vision for defence, this problem grew worse as the collective ambitions of government and the CF outstripped DND's capacity and resources.

However, as time passed, events drove a refinement of the plans for change and the likelihood of massive reduction of capability waned, at least in the short term. In addition, cognizant of the concerns of his senior leadership, the CDS, following his May 2007 G/FO Seminar, was committed to reshaping his vision to ensure that it was more inclusive. In the final analysis, guaranteeing achievability was simply not possible.

Unity and the change team. Central to General Hillier's approach was to draw like-minded people around him, people who shared his views and were not opposed to change. This initially included members of the CAT teams and then the CFTT. Subsequently, however, they increasingly were members of his key staff and trusted subordinates. This is not to say that the executive leadership team did not play a major role in CF Transformation. Indeed, many elements of change were discussed and decided at Commanders Council and Armed Forces Council. It does appear that this was not the engine of change, but rather an element of the implementation mechanism. For whatever reasons, General Hillier failed to achieve full personal buy-in from his most senior generals and admirals.

At the beginning, General Hillier attempted to engage in a dialogue and to build a collegial approach. His expectation was that there would be harmony in their perspectives. Despite an initially warm reception to his vision, the mood became skeptical. This was understandable, given the uncertainty surrounding such sensitive issues as the future of the environmental chiefs and the prospects for core capability. Equally understandable was the problem as seen from General Hillier's perspective. He saw the need to improve the capability and credibility of the CF if there was to be any hope that the government would properly resource defence. His strategy, much as for his predecessors, was to retain the best possible combat capability, structured to face the kinds of threats that he foresaw, while maintaining adequate balance as a hedge against long-term risk.

The reality was that he had no assurances from government and could not provide the senior military leadership any guarantees. The result was insufficient trust at the top to accept the risks inherent in General Hillier's vision and to buy into the change program. In such a climate, the desirable level of unity may just have been out of reach.

SUMMARY

Creating the environment for change is never easy and General Hillier had his challenges in this regard. There is no question that he communicated his vision most effectively across the CF and the nation, and this provided him with a position of credibility and strength as he moved forward with change. General Hillier clearly would have preferred a united change team at the top that embraced a common vision for the future. However, it became clear relatively early that such an objective was unlikely to be achieved, particularly in the short term. Convinced of the critical importance of achieving early gains, he took a pragmatic approach, increasingly building his efforts on the support of those who shared his vision. In tactical terms, he was prepared to "picket and bypass" opposition in order to achieve his objectives.[47]

CHAPTER 6

DEVELOPING THE STRATEGY AND PLAN

A compelling vision, communicated by a convincing leader, can launch change. People want to be part of an organization that they see as improving, and they are often energized by the promise that the vision offers. Indeed, many will see the idea as a panacea for every organizational dissatisfier. But, as the old saying goes, the devil is often in the detail, and many a change endeavour flounders due to the lack of a simple, well understood strategy and an effective, pragmatic plan.

Having developed a vision for where he wants to take the organization, the real challenge for the change leader is getting there. The leader must develop a sound strategy that factors in many dimensions of the organizational change problem and will positively shape the environment to allow real change to occur. He must also ensure the development of a plan or plans that clearly articulate the goals to be achieved and that guide the organization's actions and pacing to achieve them.

DEVELOPMENT OF THE STRATEGY

Organizational change requires a strategy that articulates not only the ends to be achieved but the ways and means of achieving them. It must take into account the magnitude of the changes to be made, the organization's ability to achieve them over time, the resources available to accomplish them and, of course, the role of both internal and external stakeholders. This strategy will be long-term and must have well defined objectives and goals, achievement of which ensures attainment of the vision. It must also contain a high degree of flexibility in approach, in order to adapt to the unforeseen but inevitable problems and changes that will occur.

Developing plans. While essential to the change process, the strategy is not sufficient in itself to guide the institution forward. Plans are required to provide the framework for the change process, identify the specific objectives and goals to be achieved, assign tasks to ensure actions to realize those goals, allocate resources, and identify the timings for actions.

Placing this planning in a DND/CF context, there are really two major purposes of the planning being undertaken. The first is the development of a strategic resource plan for government. This is a major program document that articulates what the DND/CF is to achieve and the resources it requires, as it tries to answer the question "what is the CF to be?" The second purpose is the development of an internal change implementation plan to provide the strategic/operational framework, and guidance to shape the efforts of the institution in implementing change, while continuing to conduct operations and sustain the institution. This is to be the "how" document that ensures the overall strategic coherence of the organization, and could also see a number of supporting plans being developed, focused by function (resources, personnel, equipment, etc.) or by organization.

Balancing effort. As indicated in the previous chapter, a change leader must take his time and set the conditions for successful change. This means achieving strategic coherence in his change activities, which implies the development of a coherent strategy and sufficiently detailed plans to guide change actions throughout the organization. With greater coherence and detail comes improved understanding of what the vision really means and people are better able to see themselves in the "new" organization. This should result in a greater degree of buy-in and a smoother transition to implementation.

However, development of strategic coherence and achievement of high levels of support can come at a significant cost – time! The change leader must overcome considerable inertia within the institution to achieve any change. This usually requires the leverage created by his appointment or, in some cases, unique events that have created the conditions for change. In all cases, real change must start to occur relatively early in the process if the change leader has any chance of overcoming institutional inertia. He must also be conscious of the fact that his political support is finite, and he must maintain his credibility to ensure he can continue with the required change. This means that he has to show progress relatively early.

The balance that the change leader must achieve is a difficult one and ultimately is a compromise between taking the time to undertake sufficient planning, team building, and getting on with the task of starting real change. In the final analysis, early commencement of change implementation is preferable.[48]

ASSESSMENT

Strategy. General Hillier unquestionably had a strategy that guided his efforts, although it was not written. An intuitive officer by nature, with a good strategic sense, he established strategic goals and shaped the ways of achieving them over time. The essence of the strategy was to induce fundamental change into the CF; fixing, expanding and modernizing the force, thereby making it relevant, responsive and effective, and increasing its credibility with the government and Canadians. The essential elements of the strategy included:

- Moving quickly in order to overcome institutional inertia and to counter political skepticism that the CF would be able to change;

- Implementing a new unified command and control model, as a first step, to create sufficient change to overcome resistance and to force a greater unity in operations;

- Focusing on improving operational effectiveness, leveraging the high tempo of current operations, as a means of reshaping DND/CF institutional culture; and

- Raising the credibility and value of the CF with the government and the Canadian people through improved operational effectiveness and mission success.

In effect, by focusing on command and control and operations, General Hillier intended to create pressure on other parts of the institution to change. He envisaged that the new command and control model would force a reconsideration of how all parts of the DND/CF worked together. In particular, he believed the increased focus on operations would improve the responsiveness of the institution to operational issues and shape the institutional culture, and that the greater focus on joint operations would force the environments at the operational and tactical levels to work more closely together, thus shaping CF culture and creating pressure on the strategic level for greater integration. Thus, his approach was not to attempt to plan every aspect of the change, but rather to create such pressures within the DND/CF that would force the institution to adapt.

The strategic resource plan. There were inadequate resources to achieve this strategy, and General Hillier knew that he would have to demonstrate an ability to change the CF in order for those resources to be realized. As referred to in Chapter 4, Prime Minister Martin had made it clear that a different argument for resource increases would be needed. Indeed, General Hillier anticipated that, as the ability of the CF to support national objectives increased, thereby raising its value with government and its credibility with Canadians, the resource he required to achieve his vision would materialize. While General Hillier had a strategy that he was following, the articulation of that strategy in the form of a strategic plan was not fully realized. The biggest challenge he faced was the perennial difficulty of developing a balanced, achievable and affordable plan that met the strategic requirements, could navigate the government bureaucracy, and could achieve resources and political approval.

The strategic resource plan is a relatively standard part of government programming, albeit known under a variety of different names over time. During this period, the Defence Capabilities Plan (DCP) and subsequently the *Canada First Defence Strategy* (CFDS)[49] were the latest in a long line of such strategic documents, focused on achieving a balanced strategic program that would ensure the maintenance of capability.

The CF, for many years, has grappled with the conflicting defence requirements of government. On the one hand, the government's central bureaucracy (i.e., central agencies such as the Privy Council Office and the Treasury Board) has demanded, as is reasonable, a clear long-term program plan that identifies the defence capability and structure to be sustained for the resources that government has allocated. On the other hand, there has been a desire, in particular by the government, to maintain, or to be seen to maintain, an effective military capability, for a minimum of resources invested. The central issue and the source of the dilemma facing generations of military and defence leaders has been the willingness of elected officials to adequately fund the military they want or, alternatively, to make the decisions to do away with capability they cannot or will not afford. This, of course, is an issue that has been, and probably will be, debated forever and cannot be divorced from the classic "guns or butter" argument. But, the root of the problem in Canada is a fundamental lack of understanding within government of the costs of defence capability, combined with a belief that the country is not at risk and therefore does not need to invest in this capability.

Through this period, the DND/CF faced this old problem but in a new context. A new defence policy, with a vision for a transformed CF, had been developed and approved by Prime Minister Martin's government and the CF was in the throes of change. However, while increased funding for DND was clearly in the cards, it is equally clear that the real cost of this new vision was not well understood, if indeed it was even known. As the work to develop the DCP progressed, and the magnitude of the new initiatives became clear, it became apparent that the cost of the defence program was far higher than had been anticipated. This made the challenge of fitting the essential defence capabilities into an affordable program and plan much more difficult.

It also made for a challenging political issue. In recent years, all governments have wanted to be seen to increase defence capability, and this became particularly so with the arrival of the Conservative government. In fairness, there were significant new dollars promised for defence, a commitment to purchase significant new operational capabilities (strategic lift, medium lift helicopters, etc.) and to implement an expansion of the CF. However, there is often a political price to be paid for too much defence spending and the government seemed inclined to aim for a military that would express satisfaction with the resources provided. So, the debate over resources became a major source of the frustration, as the department attempted to harmonize the conflicting issues and achieve an affordable plan that would realize the vision.

In developing the program, DND had to consider the balancing of overall capability requirements in the context of the approved and, at times changing, defence policy. This led, inevitably, to DND considering not only what new capabilities would be required, but what old capabilities could or should be divested. Such options are not relished by the defence leadership but, given the resource shortfall, they had to be presented. However, it is equally clear that such thoughts were politically unpalatable, as no government wants to be seen to reduce capability, especially when they have campaigned on increasing support to defence. The result was an impasse through much of this period as the leadership and government debated how to cut the defence cloth to meet the nation's needs.

The implications of this lack of an approved, coherent strategic resource plan, while not new, were significant for General Hillier's plans for transformation. Practically speaking, the lack of an approved plan created significant resource pressures that impacted all parts of the institution. Finding the resources to restructure the CF, fund major new capital projects, expand the CF and conduct major operations, all while sustaining the historic core military capabilities, became visibly impractical, and created a perception and a reality of shortage (dollars, people, equipment), in a time when the expectations of the vision would lead people to believe the situation would improve. However, more fundamentally, the lack of clarity created a large and growing concern amongst many of the senior leaders as to the CF's ability to maintain the core capability. Each leader in his stead, expressed concerns, publicly and privately, about the erosion of capability in the short term and the potential for loss of specific capabilities in the longer term. The result of all this was an erosion of belief in the viability of the vision.

Internal change plans. While an approved strategic resource plan was important for DND/CF, in some ways, the internal change plan was more significant for the institution. After all, a coherent internal plan was vital for managing the change being undertaken in order to minimize the turmoil inherent in the change process. This was particularly important given the lack of cohesion in the recommendations and approaches taken by the respective CATs.

There were attempts to create such plans. During its time, the CFTT developed an outline transformation road map that was to have been a guide to the change being planned. However, it never reached maturity and, when the team was disbanded, for all practical purposes, it ceased to exist. In 2005, DGSP assembled a small team to undertake campaign planning, in parallel to the development of the DCP. The intent was to develop a coherent campaign plan for mapping out the implementation goals and actions, and to guide decision-making. However, as progress on the DCP faltered, this work was put into abeyance and was never finalized. As a consequence, no campaign plan, or similar plan to guide transformation implementation, currently exists.

It was argued that lack of such a plan was primarily due to the lack of a strategic resource plan and that, once it had been completed, the campaign plan would have flowed from it. While logical in terms of transformation process, it ignored the fundamental requirement for the institution to ensure coherence and understanding in its actions. There is no doubt that the leadership would never consider launching a major operation without a plan to guide all involved, but that is in effect what happened in terms of transforming the CF. So, while the vision was out there, and many written and verbal directions for change existed, no one document was available that gave people a coherent understanding of how it all fit together. In addition, while the Transformation directive that the CDS had signed provided broad guidance, it did not specifically assign objectives to subordinates and it left unanswered the question of implementation of many of the CAT recommendations. Lacking a top-down assignment of synchronized objectives, the new commanders were building their concept of operations (CONOPS) and the required structure to implement them bottom up. The resultant uncoordinated operational command CONOPS and the heavy demand for officers to fill the redundant joint staff functions appears to have been a major contributor to an increasingly strong perception that Transformation was unaffordable.

Resource planning — promises and assumptions. This lack of plans was critical with respect to resource planning. Unlike in the tactical and operational domains, strategic resource planning requires discipline and a long-term perspective. Undertaking such a massive change strategy, which included major re-capitalization, demands large amounts of money.

While the CDS had predicated some of his ambition on gaining more resources, he could not spend what he did not have. This meant that, at least in the short term, he required an innovative resource strategy that provided him with the resources he needed to get transformation underway and meet the growing demands, while also ensuring good fiscal accountability.

Human resource planning. Arguably, more important than the availability of dollars in implementing change is the demand for human resources. All change has to be managed and implemented within the existing organizational structure, even if the new organization is expected to be larger. After all, growing an organization in human resource terms is a lengthy process and personnel availability will lag demand for some considerable time. When demand includes increases for both operations and force expansion, the human resource issue becomes critical, potentially jeopardizing the change initiative.

In this event, the resource and human resource strategies were shrouded in some uncertainty. Clearly not enough money existed to achieve the vision, a reality that became clear to government by 2006. In addition, the human resource demands were taxing the institution, and balancing the growing demands against a limited supply required great deftness. Unquestionably, the CDS was following a "managed risk" resource strategy with the intent to reduce demand and increase supply as the various transformation initiatives matured. However, given the lack of a coherent plan for implementation of change, it is unclear how the resource and personnel staffs would be able to maintain a sound approach and manage that risk as it grew.

There may be many reasons for this oversight. Certainly, there were pressures on all involved. In particular, the capacity of the small core planning staffs within the VCDS Group collectively was a serious limitation. However, there is likely a more philosophical issue at the root of the approach taken. General Hillier applied his operational orientation to the problem of change with much good effect, but one probable factor is that he overestimated the ability of an operational approach to command to be effective in a corporate environment. He had imparted his intent to the senior leadership of the CF and had done superb work in verbally communicating his vision to many throughout both the CF and DND. His command-centric approach to addressing many of the issues was quite effective. In particular, the speed and effectiveness with which he created the operational commands is a testament to the strength of that approach. By providing those commanders with his intent and ensuring oversight on their implementation, the stand-up of those organizations, albeit at times chaotic, was achieved in a remarkably short period of time and in a most effective manner.

Unlike an operational formation that is designed to be constantly reshaped or task-organized, however, the institutional components of the CF and DND are very rigid and inherently fragile. This fragility had in fact been increased in previous years through the restructuring and "downsizing" of many parts of the organization. As a consequence, the rapid and major restructuring of DND/CF saw a fundamental shift in many of the responsibility centres that resulted in a fracturing of some of the well-established processes. Added to this, the shortage of personnel, exacerbated by the growth of new capabilities such as the commands, reduced the capacity of organizations to meet their mandates. This meant that corporate functions, essential to keeping the institution running smoothly, became unbalanced and placed increasing demands on leaders and managers to keep shoring up the dikes.

All change is limited by the organization's capacity. But, the dominant factor in maximizing capacity and ensuring successful change is good management. In the case of CF Transformation, the real problem has been a lack of common understanding and good coordination. There has been no plan to guide the internal changes and many of the decisions required for adapting the institution to maintain cohesion. The demands of four new operational commands and a high level of operations, increasingly generated with no forewarning, resulted in a reactionary approach within the force generators and the corporate centre, increasing fragmentation of process and further reducing cohesion. This, combined with a general lack of understanding at lower levels on the intent or philosophy they should follow in reshaping the institution, meant decisions were being made in isolation, with no understanding of the impact elsewhere in the system, and no ability to coordinate them.

SUMMARY

The genius of General Hillier's strategy for implementing change within the CF was to move quickly, to take risks, and to manage such risks through adjustments. By unseating resistance and forcing fundamental change, he could more easily shape the institution and its culture to his needs. However, the effect of this rapid, and at times chaotic, change was to create a degree of turmoil that came close to overwhelming the institution. Large, rapid changes inevitably create a tumultuous environment and place increasing demands on leaders and staffs throughout the organization to manage the chaos and to mitigate the negative consequences of the changes. This is not a new problem, especially for a profession whose role is the management of violence in an environment of chaos. However, in order to lead and manage in such an environment, there needs to be a clear intent and at least an outline plan to guide the many different parts of the organization.

The work by the CF on the many different plans was an attempt to bring coherence to the evolving strategy and provide a clear framework to guide transformation. Despite all this effort, no plan was finalized or approved, but the progressive work on these plans had its benefits. The result was an enhanced understanding among senior leaders that allowed the institution to adapt to the changing requirements. Indeed, elements of this planning found their way into the CDS' thinking and, indeed, into his directions for the future. Nonetheless, the principle consequence was a lack of strategic coherence in the organization of change. While the senior leadership had a sense of what they were trying to achieve, the inter-relationships and the second- and third-order effects of any decisions were often less than clear, resulting in a lack of clarity and understanding within the DND/CF on the direction of change, and an erosion of trust and loss of credibility in the Transformation program. It also placed great pressure on senior staffs to coordinate issues and to ensure risks were adequately managed.

To some extent, this problem was not one of the CF's making. The inability to achieve agreement on some very difficult political and resource issues, given the political context, was not surprising. The failure to develop coherent internal plans to guide CF Transformation is significant. If the strength of General Hillier and his team was in strategy, speed and risk taking, their weakness was the failure to develop coherent implementation plans.

CHAPTER 7

LEADING AND IMPLEMENTING CHANGE

A GENERIC OVERVIEW

Leaders are all important in organizational change. It is the change leader's vision and only he can convince others of the wisdom of that direction. But, as the leader, he must understand and manage many conflicting organizational and cultural dynamics. As with any family, change creates conflict amongst its members, each believing that change will disadvantage them over others and perceiving, in every nuance, a new threat to their future. In such an environment, the change leader must be a wise parent; guiding, encouraging, managing expectations and rewarding those who are most successful, while avoiding any favouritism. He must possess great patience!

Effecting organizational change is very much a matter of personal leadership, less concerned with providing direction and much more focused on convincing people. After all, few people want to change and, as individuals mature and are successful in their profession, their flexibility and willingness to change wanes. So, the change leader must create a personal relationship with his key subordinates and, to some degree, the whole organization. He must convince people to do what they may not like.

This is not just a matter of convincing people to change, or waiting for consensus to emerge. The change leader must possess an extremely strong will used to push the organization to change. That means making tough decisions and moving forward, sometimes in spite of others. Consensus, if necessary, but not necessarily consensus! Ideally, the doubters will see the wisdom of the approach as change is implemented, or at least will get on board with it if they do not. Otherwise, they will get left behind. Obviously, such an approach has its limits and the change leader must constantly remain alert to the dangers of the re-emergence of institutional inertia.

So, the change leader must endeavour to maintain a balance, managing the family and its constituent parts, while pushing the organization to change. To achieve this balance, he must above all maintain his credibility, that is to say his moral authority, thus ensuring that ability to continue to effect change.

Selection and maintenance of the aim. The change leader must keep his eye firmly on the objective of developing a new and better organization. His goal is not just change but a new and better capability. He must see the change dynamic as a means to an end. There will be no end of challenges thrown at him during the change period, and many "nay sayers" will attempt to detract him. He must stay the course.

Focus on leading. It is vital that the change leader focus on leading, keeping to the strategic issues, and not getting bogged down in the details of running the organization or of change. This means that he needs an effective management team to address these matters for him and must have the confidence to let them do the job. He remains accountable and must maintain sufficient oversight in order to retain a good sense of the organization's cohesion and capacity. In this way, his decisions will be founded in a solid understanding of what the institution can do.

Ensuring understanding and motivating the team. A large part of the change leader's role must be a motivational one. It is his vision and he is responsible for achieving it and making the organization better. He must demonstrate that sense of ownership to his people at all levels – in short, he must be the face of the institution.

In this context, communication becomes one of his major priorities. It is said that the three most important activities when implementing change within an organization are communication, communication and communication! Such an expression illustrates the reality that ensuring understanding of any initiative in large organizations is challenging, especially given the effect of informal communication or rumour that distorts the intent, often portraying the outcome in negative terms. The change leader must recognize this and ensure that his message is getting out to all parts of the organization.

Accurate, relevant information is vital to any organization undergoing change. People need to be kept informed, to understand the details of the change strategy, and to plan as they unfold. They need to know not only where the organization is going, but also where they are in the change process, what initiatives are being undertaken, and why and whether they are being successful. They also need opportunities to have their concerns and questions dealt with. After all, there will be great concern, even fear during the change process, and every effort must be taken to implement a communications strategy to support the change initiative.

Sustaining change leader credibility. Throughout the process, the change leader must maintain a clear sense of his credibility. It is this almost intangible element of how he is seen both internally and externally that provides him the latitude to decide or act, and it ultimately allows him to sustain change. As long as the leader is trusted and believed, much can be overlooked or forgiven but, if that credibility erodes, he will quickly lose the people and the organization. In short, it is his currency to spend or to waste. If he has it, he can overcome great obstacles. If he does not have it, no amount of effort will see success. This requires him to know himself, his strengths and weaknesses.

To maintain his credibility, the change leader must build on those strengths. The evolving plans must take his credibility into account and may need to be shaped in a manner that ensures it, implying that sound and balanced decision-making is an important component of the strategy. Decisions must not only be sound but must be seen to be sound if the institution and the change leader are to remain credible.

Clearly, communication plays a large role in sustaining that credibility as the change leader's ideas and persona are projected to the organization, but it also depends on the overall credibility of the change program. In essence, if people cannot make sense of the changes being undertaken, no amount of personal charisma will keep the people with him.

Self-confidence. It is critical that the strategic leader have a high degree of self-confidence. That is not to say that he should be so confident as to be reckless, but he must trust in his abilities and, in particular, his sense of what is right and what is possible. He must take risks and cannot take counsel of his fears.

ASSESSMENT OF THE CHANGE LEADER

General Hillier's focus was leading the CF through change. Given his operational pedigree, he had no difficulty in leaving the details to his subordinates. Indeed, he had great trust in his VCDS, Vice-Admiral Ronald Buck, and relied heavily on him to coordinate the details while he, as CDS, focused on leading. He clearly understood the importance of effective communication and spent a large part of his busy schedule communicating, both publicly and privately, using his personal skills to great effect. Indeed, the CDS' ability to "speak" to people was the cornerstone of his personal credibility and an integral part of the current high profile of the CF. He was most effective in articulating the vision, convincing and energizing the members of the CF, as well as the Canadian public. The General from Newfoundland became standard fare in the newspapers and on radio and television across the country.

Although General Hillier's credibility was high, support for his vision was not unanimous. While the CDS had early strong support amongst his officers, concerns persisted amongst the senior leadership and staff over the inclusiveness and achievability of the vision, the resource pressures, personnel tempo and overall sustainability of the CF. Not surprisingly, those who had to play the greatest roles in managing these risks have harboured the greatest concerns. Probably, the greatest factor in their level of disquiet was that the environment was becoming chaotic and that people were losing their frames of reference essential to guiding them on a daily basis.

Unquestionably, General Hillier's personal communications had been most effective. However, it would appear that much of the communications activities had been generated on an opportunity basis and there had not been an effective communications strategy or plan to support Transformation. The result had been that the institution had not kept its members abreast of the changes planned or educated them well on the state of Transformation. It is instructive that, since embarking on the transformation of the CF, a period approaching three years, the CDS had only issued a total of five public situational reports (SITREPS) on change. This tendency to "under communicate" was often the critical shortcoming in organizational change attempts and this may very well have been the case with the CF. While many had heard the CDS speak at "town halls" on the broad aspects of Transformation, the details of change had not been well communicated.

Finally, General Hillier maintained his aura of confidence and his reputation as a risk taker. While any leader has periods of self doubt, it would appear that, from a personal perspective, General Hillier weathered a very difficult period well. This permitted him to sustain his high risk approach, which clearly created problems for others, but it allowed him to make advances where no one else could.

General Hillier had initiated the leadership of the CF through Transformation. In so doing, he was practicing his own philosophy of "command centricity", relying heavily on his leadership team and placing his emphasis where it should be, on the critical strategic leadership issues. Through it all, he maintained his focus, his confidence and his credibility, becoming the very face of Transformation.

GENERIC CHALLENGES IN IMPLEMENTING CHANGE

Surveys show that 70% to 90% of organizations fail to successfully execute their strategies. In most cases, the failure is one of execution, not the strategy itself. Our own research traces this failure to two causes. Since there is no generally accepted way to describe a strategy, organizations are attempting to execute something that isn't even articulated. The second is that management systems aren't linked to organizational strategy. If the primary drivers of organizational change do not focus on the strategy, successful execution is impossible.[50]

In order to realize his vision, the change leader must understand and shape many individual and collective dynamics within the organization, and develop a clear strategy and a coherent plan to guide the institution forward. Only by executing his plans effectively can his vision be achieved, and it is here that the greatest challenges are faced.

When executing change, the change leader must overcome the resistance to change or inertia within the organization and get people moving. Once he has achieved a degree of forward momentum his problems have just begun, for he must ensure the effective management of change by shaping the institution for change, coordinating the many elements of change, and constantly balancing the vision and objectives with resource available. This must recognize that change will create a significant increase in workload in the short term, requiring the organization to adapt to that additional load and the requirements of managing the many change initiatives. Once the organization is moving and change has started producing some results, there is a danger in assuming that the task will be easy. However, it is here in sustaining change that the greatest effort is required. To maintain the momentum gained, the change leader must empower a broad-based action and adjust to changing requirements. This also requires the maintenance of credibility by demonstrating success, consolidating gains and building on those gains.

Overcoming inertia. When introducing change, leaders face resistance that can effectively kill the transformation before it gets started. Many people are comfortable with the organization as it is and see no advantage and considerable risk in changing it. Indeed, many will see in the change program real threats, not only to the institution, but to themselves. The result can be numerous people who consciously, or even subconsciously, fight the directed changes. Faced with this challenge, the change leader must devise strategies and actions to overcome the inertia of institutional resistance and to maintain the momentum once started.

Organizing for change. The first step in setting the conditions for success is recognition that the institution is not capable of implementing major change, and continuing to meet its mission, without adjusting the organization to meet these new and larger demands. There are many models to follow in this regard and no one correct solution, however there are some clear principles that must be followed.

First, the change leader must continue to lead the change. This is his vision and plan, and his presence and involvement is essential throughout the change process. It requires a careful re-prioritizing of the change leader's time and activities to ensure that, despite the other pressures, he maintains effective leadership of the change initiative.

Second, there must be a senior executor of change with the requisite authority and an appropriate staff to plan and oversee the implementation of change. This change executor is not, and cannot be, a replacement for the change leader. But, there are limits to what the change leader can do and he requires assistance in ensuring effective coordination and sustainment of the change initiative. The change executor must have the full trust of, and be able to speak for, the change leader. Indeed, he must be in the mind of the change leader at all times and there must never be a perceived difference in interpretation of the way ahead.

Third, there must be a reordering of priorities and tasks assigned to senior leaders and organizations. Change demands more effort, but effective implementation cannot be achieved by hard work alone. The reality is that, during a period of change, something must give and the senior leadership must make the hard decisions on what will be sidelined for later. In addition, all must be clear about the priorities and placement of the change management tasks in the overall order of things. This is particularly so for the executor of change, and one of the key decisions must be whether this is created as a new position or assumed by one of the existing senior leaders (usually the Chief Operating Officer or Chief of Staff). If it is the latter, his responsibilities must be seriously restructured to ensure that change receives the appropriate priority and attention.

Finally, there must be an agreed upon, well-understood and utilized process by which change is managed and issues are coordinated and deconflicted. Change must become a major business line within the organization, with a clear and effective governance structure and an effective management staff to plan and coordinate implementation. In particular, the efforts of the change team must be closely coordinated with the routine organizational activity and the corporate management schedule adjusted accordingly.

Balancing of vision and resources. Implementing major structural change requires the development of a whole new organization that must be planned, resourced and built. At the same time, the existing structure must prepare for and support the change, while continuing to conduct its responsibilities. The transfer of responsibilities to the new organization can be done in small evolutionary steps or in large revolutionary leaps. This often requires reorganization of the existing structure, sometimes several times, as it adapts to its changing tasks and resource base. The latter is most demanding, for the demand for greater numbers of people stretches the personnel resources available over a much larger structure. Even if the new model is no more resource intensive, the transition period will stretch the systems capacity.

Coordinating change. Maintaining organizational cohesion during change, especially in a complex government structure, is most challenging, as an organization requires not only good leadership but superb coordination of that change to realize its aims. Change fractures the traditional organizational structures and processes, which are the body and life blood of the institution, requiring all parts of the organization to adapt. It is therefore essential that the exact nature and timing of structural and process changes be closely coordinated in order to minimize disruption. Knowledge is crucial and all parts of the organization must know where to go to ascertain the state of change and authoritative information on the processes to be followed.

Sustaining change. Once the change leader has achieved a degree of forward momentum within the organization, his problems have just begun. At every turn, he will encounter obstacles that will delay or derail his plans and potentially erode confidence. He therefore needs to consider actions and strategies that allow him to sustain change over the long haul, maintaining momentum, adjusting to the unforeseen and maintaining credibility in the change process. Perhaps, the most important of these is the maintenance of the momentum of change. This is less a specific action than a general state or dynamic that requires a delicate balance of factors that ensure the continuation of the change program. On the one hand, it means the progressive, physical change of the organization, in line with the vision that demonstrates that the program is working and that each day sees a move closer to the promised future. On the other hand, it means the maintenance of the credibility of the change program by ensuring engagement of all members of the organization and the continued commitment of the leadership to what they have started.

Adjusting to changing requirements. The challenges of organizational change cannot be considered in isolation, but must take into account the continuing demands of running the business. After all, change is a means to an end and the change program cannot be allowed to jeopardize the effectiveness of the organization. This means that change must weather a storm of unforeseen circumstances, requiring adjustments of the change program while balancing the other organizational requirements. The change team must be flexible in their approach while maintaining a determination that change will proceed.

Consolidating gains and producing more change. Achieving fundamental change takes a long time, and sustaining the required focus over the long haul is difficult. Given human nature, people seek stability and want to put the turmoil and difficulties of organizational change behind them. It is easy then for any initial success to be considered the end of the problem, and people lean toward declaring victory, when in fact the organizational change has barely started. Change leaders must therefore capitalize on successes to consolidate their effort, but use these successes as platforms for further change. In this manner, leaders celebrate the successes, giving credit where it is due, but maintain the momentum for the long term.

Empowering broad-based action. Real change cannot be achieved by one person alone, but demands the genuine commitment of a hard core of change leaders. Increasingly, it must be embraced by people at all levels of the organization. This demands that people throughout the organization be empowered to take reasonable action in line with the change vision. Indeed, all within the organization must take ownership of the change vision and program. In some regards, this can be accomplished by a broad philosophy, implicit within the vision, but often it requires specific direction and action to get people to act on their own initiative.

In considering the empowerment of his people, the change leader must ensure two things. First, he must be confident that those he is empowering understand his intent in sufficient detail to ensure that they will act in line with the philosophy he is espousing. In this regard, the use of broad principles, clearly articulated throughout the organization, is most valuable. Next, he must impart a commitment that gives the empowered the confidence to act. This will be the most difficult to address as the strength of the existing culture will act as a barrier or impediment to any alternative behaviours. The change leader must ensure they are given permission to act. Sustaining or focusing that knowledge and confidence then becomes one of the change leader's principle foci, for it is this empowered body that ultimately will ensure he reaches his goal.

Maintaining credibility. The change leader must think in terms of maintaining credibility, which must be a central theme of his transformation planning and communication. Sustaining change is in large measure about keeping the trust of the people. If the overall approach is credible, the result is a degree of trust amongst the people that buys time, allowing the change program to mature. Such credibility depends, in part, on the strategic coherence of the change initiative, but the leader needs to show that change is working and can improve the organization. The generation of short-term wins that demonstrate not only that change is possible, but also that it can improve the organization, is essential early in the program. Such successes must continue to be achieved to avoid the loss of support.

ASSESSMENT

As one would expect, the implementation of CF Transformation was an extremely dynamic process. Driven as he was by circumstances to move quickly, General Hillier knew that he would have to sort out much of the detail of change once it was underway. This placed a great deal on his shoulders and that of his principal subordinates as they were required to maintain a close watch on implementation. But, this fluid environment fit well with his command-centric philosophy and personal style.

Creating irreversible momentum. Key to implementation of his change plans, General Hillier saw the need to overcome institutional inertia and, as he put it, "to create irreversible momentum". He believed that, while the structural changes inherent in the implementation of a new command and control model would create significant turmoil, they would also unseat the sources of resistance. He saw the establishment of the operational commands outside of NDHQ and the coincident dissolution of the DCDS group, as eliminating the traditional operations staff matrix within NDHQ. In its place, the driver for operations would rest primarily with four operational commanders, all responsible to the CDS and all following a command-centric philosophy.

There is no question that this created the dynamic that the CDS wished. With the stand up of the operational commanders and the disappearance of the DCDS, the operational influence within the CF moved outside of NDHQ. At the same time, the power of the traditional staff matrix was dispersed and the vast majority of the effort was focused on making the new system work. In short, people didn't have the organizational focus or the time to fight the problem.

Of course, one of the consequences of this dynamic, given the late stand up of the SJS and the CFTT, was a reduction in strategic control. The operational commanders had a relatively free hand for quite some time before CT and SJS Director of Staff (DOS) started to impose a degree of oversight on all that was happening. But, as important as it was for starting change, this "constructive chaos" created a growing concern amongst many who saw it as a dangerous loss of cohesion in an institution that was already fragile.

Managing change. From the outset, General Hillier knew he needed a capable change management team and in particular a solid change executor. Faced with growing demands for senior leaders and seeking an appropriate executor, he selected MGen Walter Natynczyk, an officer he knew well and in whom he had great trust, as the Chief of Transformation.

The CF Transformation Team was established as quickly as possible under MGen Natynczyk's leadership, but clearly late to the need. It undertook the essential analysis to drive implementation of CF Transformation and, under the circumstances, did a good job of coordinating change initiatives.

However, MGen Natynczyk faced conditions that did not set him up well for success.

Until early 2005, MGen Natynczyk had been serving outside the country and had little recent knowledge of events within the CF. While he had served as director of operations within the DCDS Group in the late 1990s, he had no recent experience in NDHQ. Finally, his relatively junior status as a general officer placed hurdles in front of him. He had to come up to speed on a very complex undertaking, establish his presence within the headquarters and in particular with the senior leadership, and establish a degree of control on a change process in which most were already well ahead of him.

Once he gained a degree of control in the change file in summer 2005, he recognized that he needed an effective governance structure and change coordination capability. During 2005, he focused on structuring the CFTT to handle the key elements of the task (Planning, Realignment, Coordination and Analysis) and developed a governance structure that provided him with the ability to shape strategic issues with the senior leadership, while harmonizing the more detailed elements of the task at the senior staff level. The senior organization, the Transformation Steering Group (TSG) had membership at the Level 1 and was focused on providing guidance on all transformation initiatives, which in turn were passed before AFC. This was supported by the TSAT, with representatives from across the staff matrix focused on developing options and coordinating Transformation activities. While this in time became effective, the improvement was short-lived. As soon as the decision was made to stand up the operational headquarters on 1 February 2006, the effort on this all-important task waned and the capacity of the CFTT started to erode. The consequence was little effective central staff coordination and management of the change initiative. Then, having just reached its stride, the decision was taken in June 2006 to disband the CFTT team and manage Transformation from within the existing command structure. This meant, in practice, oversight by then-LGen Natynczyk, the VCDS, through his key staffs, the Chief of Force Development (CFD) and the Chief of Program (CProg). However, these two organizations were just being re-created with elements having previously been part of DGSP. The transformation function was quickly absorbed into the staff structure and coordination assigned to COS Transformation, a colonel who reported directly to the VCDS.

It is clear that, despite good intentions, the objective to create an effective organization to plan and manage change was never fully realized. The turmoil created by the lateness of the decision to create the CFTT, the limited time it was in existence and the subsequent internal changes to the VCDS Group, detracted from the cohesion required to manage change effectively. While many good people worked very hard to achieve the objective, the reality is that the task was beyond them. The forces of change had been unleashed and the limited staff dedicated to coordinating and managing Transformation had neither the capacity nor the influence to get those change forces under control.

The reality is that Transformation was command-led and, given the pace of change, the organizational management never caught up. The result was increased turmoil and lack of coherence. That is not to say that the senior leadership did not focus on the matter; indeed the CDS, the VCDS and others spent a great deal of effort in trying to achieve a degree of strategic coherence. However, such coherence cannot be achieved from the top alone, and an effective management and coordination staff is essential to implementing change in an organization of the size and complexity of the CF.

Success in managing change must also be seen from the perspective of all that the DND/CF had to accomplish. The reality is that the institution faced a considerable number of significant challenges, some of them unforeseen, that forced adjustments to change plans. Unquestionably, the greatest impact came from the increase in operational tempo that, in both military and political terms, placed a great load on the senior leadership. This was exacerbated by increased resource pressures and the shortage of people that, probably more than any other factor, limited the achievement of all of the CF's objectives. Finally, one cannot ignore the significant impact of a change of government in January 2006, with a different vision of where it wanted the CF to go. These, combined with the demands of structural change, placed a tremendous load on the institution. The fact that CF Transformation was able to adjust to the changing requirements, and achieve as much as it did through this period, is remarkable in itself. It is a testament to the leadership and the staffs that made it happen.

The balancing of vision and resources. As often happens in major organizational change, the CF experienced difficulties in the balancing of the demands of implementing change with the resources available. By mid-October 2005, the plans for implementing the operational headquarters were well advanced. It was becoming increasingly clear that, for a variety of reasons, resource limitations were causing difficulties in the establishment of these headquarters, while maintaining the rest of the structure. While to some degree an inevitable outcome of change, it became apparent that the demands being put forward by these new commands were greater than had been forecast. The problem was identified by the CFTT, but attempts to resolve the matter were unsuccessful.

At its root was a difference of philosophy on how these new headquarters were to operate. The CDS' guidance had been that command headquarters would to a large extent share resources, building on common capabilities, thus maintaining efficiency while improving effectiveness.[51] In reality, the designated operational commanders took an approach that demanded more dedicated resources in accordance with what they perceived was required to meet their considerable responsibilities. This new resource demand was significant, and some considered them to be empire-building. In reality, the truth probably lay somewhere in between. The result, for a long time, was an impasse with commanders insisting that they needed more people and refusing to change the operational concept upon which their headquarters operated. This led to the CDS directing a major functional review to harmonize requirements and to improve efficiency.[52] The results have seen an improvement in resource efficiency, but have also seen a greater level of command and control overhead than had originally been envisaged. In the final analysis, this was a consequence of a lack of clear understanding of the CDS' concept of operations and an inability of the strategic level to maintain control of the operational commanders. Overall, there was some resolution of the problems but short of that sought by the CDS.

Many saw this battle as a clear indication that the operational commands were not affordable and their existence would result in a serious degradation of the overall capability of the CF. Whether this indeed is the reality remains to be seen. What is clear is that the implementation of change was undertaken with a less than complete personnel resource plan to support implementation. To be fair, this was in large measure due to the lack of a coherent implementation plan. But the consequence was a reactionary approach to staffing change, affecting every part of the organization. Unforecast demand for personnel to meet increasing requirements stripped large numbers of staff out of existing structures, unbalancing them and creating some chaos. For a culture that abhors uncertainty, this was proof of the madness Transformation represented. It convinced many that it would not last.

Empowerment. General Hillier believed that the success of CF Transformation would depend very much on the members of the CF who would embrace his vision and philosophy for change. He tried to create this dynamic through regular and extensive communication of his vision, so that all understood where he wanted to go. By publishing his CDS Principles, he wanted to encapsulate the basic philosophy of change that he wanted embraced.

The effects of General Hillier's approach were inconsistent with respect to its reception and its effectiveness across the levels and functions of the organization. At the tactical level, given the increased emphasis on operational effectiveness, most saw the changes as positive and were eager to embrace them. At the operational level, the new commands were focused on change and pursued it with vigour. At the strategic level, the engagement was arguably less, and here, depending on which part of the organization, one could find resistance and a traditional hierarchical approach. As one senior officer said, "The troops get it; the problem is with the generals."

Credibility. The state of credibility of the CF Transformation is very much a mixed bag. As the centrepiece of the CDS' vision, the new C2 structure was put in place quickly and was effective. Indeed, this was accomplished in remarkable time and, despite the risks, without any major problems. While neither simple nor tidy, the transition was successful and the new structure stands as a testament to the CDS' determination. Although not a universal view, many observers believe the new structure, in particular the new operational commands, has proven itself, albeit efficiency remains an issue.

However, not all change was uniformly positive nor were all attempts to change successful. For example, the creation of the operational commands, while successful, was a costly undertaking and many members questioned whether their value to the restructured CF was sufficient, given the personnel costs. Critics argued that such an expense could not be justified in a small military. Equally difficult, the suspension of the SCTF, the flagship of CF Transformation, was a blow to the CDS and the credibility of the vision he espoused. He had placed great value on the demonstration of a truly joint capability and, as with his approach to operations, utilized this experiment as a means of drawing the environments closer together. In reality, however, "ends" can be attained in a variety of "ways" and the loss of one way does not negate, nor make impossible, the importance or achievability of the objective. The challenge that this has posed for the CDS however, is how he is to establish the culture he seeks and to minimize the impact of this SCTF loss on the credibility of Transformation. The success or failure of specific elements of change may, in the final analysis, be less important than the overall sense of progress, and that clearly varies depending on where one sits. The reality is that, for the majority of the CF, the changes have been positive and are seen as such.

SUMMARY

With the stand up of the operational commands, the major objectives of Phase 2 of the CDS' Transformation plan effectively had been achieved, albeit there remained many details to finalize. Given the challenge faced by the CF, General Hillier saw this as an appropriate time to consolidate work on Transformation, based very much on the validation reports, prior to proceeding with the third phase. As indicated earlier, this has in fact resulted in a more broad-based implementation of changes envisaged for

Phases 3 and 4. However, the principal effort for the past year, 2007, has been consolidation of the changes made.

At the time of writing, late 2007 and early 2008, this transformation consolidation phase remains ongoing and may very well determine the long-term success of CF Transformation overall. As time passes, however, without significant new change initiatives, there is an increased likelihood that all will consider any further change unnecessary and, therefore, Transformation to be seen as completed.

CHAPTER 8

SHAPING THE ORGANIZATION FOR THE LONG TERM

While the change leader will concentrate to a large degree on the immediate aspects of change, he must also maintain a watchful eye on the long term. If his efforts are to prove successful, it is in the long term that they will reach full maturity. He must therefore consider the factors that will shape this longer-term situation and how he can best influence them.

Shaping culture. The change leader must seriously consider how he will shape the culture of the organization. Culture is the way we do things and, in organizations with strong cultures, "the way we do things" becomes "who we are". When faced with a threat of change, organizations with such strong cultures see the threat not just to the organizational structure but to their very sense of self-worth within the organization. Consequently, changing this culture becomes the most important aspect of any transformation initiative.

Unfortunately, culture is not easily or directly changed and can only be shaped by small steps over time. This is best accomplished by adjusting "how things are done" to better reflect the kinds of behaviours expected in the new culture. This means leaders must state clearly which behaviours are expected, then practise them personally as an example to all of their importance, observe the emergent behaviours within the organization, and reward and correct them as necessary. The critical element is practise, as no amount of talk will change anything. Only action will be effective.

Succession planning. The change leader must recognize that transforming a large institution like the CF cannot be done overnight. Realistically, it usually cannot be done during the tenure of one leader. While it is difficult to establish specific times within which real change will be achieved, it is reasonable to think in generational terms. A wholesale change of the senior leadership of the institution is required before the underlying culture has changed sufficiently that major reversion has been avoided. In this context, one should think in terms of a decade or more to effect change.

Given this reality, the change leader must consider carefully the shaping of the leadership team, such that the new team that he will pass on to his successor is sound and will continue his work to achieve the vision. This implies not only careful selection of leaders for promotion and employment in key positions, but the development over time of the next generation of leaders. This effort will take a considerable amount of the change leader's time.

This work must also recognize that the change leader's successor will come from this group and that the institution needs several leaders in succession with a shared vision and, in general, a similar approach to realizing that vision. This means that the visionary leader, as he looks long-term, must consider not only what he can accomplish during his time in office, but who should follow him. Given a regular tour of duty as CDS of between three and five years, it would require three successive CDS with a similar vision and philosophy, if the original change objectives were to be achieved.

CONCEPTUAL AND DOCTRINAL DEVELOPMENT

Change should not be a one-time affair, but should lead to a forward-looking institutional culture where change is forecast and planned. Once implementation of the change initiative starts in earnest, the majority of the effort and time will be focused on relatively near-term issues. If there is not a conscious effort to address the longer term, there is a danger that this shorter focus will result, over time, in a loss of momentum and an acceptance that the change already achieved is sufficient. In short, this means pouring concrete around the marginal gains made and re-solidifying the change resistant culture.

To avoid this loss of momentum, the change leader must ensure that resources and time are set aside to focus on longer-term planning. This should normally be done through the mechanism of conceptual and doctrinal development that logically focuses on the changing nature of the profession. Such effort should not just be left to lower level staffs but must be personally led by the change leader. In this way, he ensures that the organization is continuing to advance its thinking, in turn shaping the near-term change initiatives and sustaining the impetus to change.

ASSESSMENT

General Hillier's philosophy in achieving the integrated CF culture that he envisioned was to push parts of the organization together, preferably in an operational setting, to create the dynamic for developing a CF culture. He had a firm belief that by doing this, people would grow together. To achieve this, he sought ways of increasing the presence of all three environments in Afghanistan, created the operational commands and joint regional headquarters, which were all joint, and commenced the creation of the SCTF, a standing joint capability. While the latter was ultimately not achieved, the remainder certainly has started the dynamic. Only time will tell whether the objective will be achieved.

Another key component of changing the culture was the publishing of the CDS' Six Principles of CF Transformation.[53] These were envisaged as philosophical guide posts or statements of expectation of organizational behaviour to guide Transformation. The CDS stated that they:

> ....are intended to guide commanders and staffs as they execute transformation activities. They are not dogmatic and no principle supersedes another. Judgment must be exercised in their use however they articulate a perspective that should routinely inform on-going analysis and decision-making. In the longer term, these principles will help re-shape and renew CF culture, creating a shared ethos fundamental to the creation of a CF that is relevant, responsive and effective in an increasingly unstable and volatile strategic environment.

The principles and definitions as published, with a full analysis of them, can be found at Annex A. In summary, they are:

- **Canadian Forces Identity**. This principle entreated all members to focus on the higher loyalty to the nation, to put environmental differences aside and build an integrated CF culture. An essential principle given his objective that would be achieved operationally through a joint command and control structure. Its application in the corporate sphere is questionable.

- **Command Centric Imperative**. Command centricity is intended to reassert the rightful place of commanders at the centre of the staff process and is at the core of the CDS' command philosophy. Its application in an operational context has merit; however it has limits when applied in a corporate setting. There have been concerns over the application of the principle by some commanders and staffs based on a questionable understanding of the concept.

- **Authorities, Responsibilities and Accountabilities**. This principle intends to establish clear command accountabilities and responsibilities rather than staff matrices, emphasizing the responsibility of commanders to ensure understanding of direction and intent.

- **Operational Focus**. The principle is focused on priorities and emphasizes an operational focus rather than the existing institutional focus. It has seen the re-emergence of a dominant operational culture within DND but it also has highlighted concerns over the potential neglect of longer-term planning, especially when the CF is facing the pressure of a high operational tempo.

- **Mission Command**. Mission Command emphasizes a culture of empowerment and a willingness to take risks. It is most appropriate for the operational culture, but of questionable usefulness in the corporate sphere.

- **An Integrated Regular, Reserve and Civilian CF**. In some respects, this is an elaboration of the first principle. It takes the ideal of "jointness" further in endeavouring to remove all barriers between organizations and people. Overcoming the cultural impediments will take time.

Conceptually, the approach of using principles to guide action is excellent, but it is not without its dangers in implementation. First and foremost, the principles must be well understood in order for the desired behaviour to be produced. This is a concern and there are clear examples of even senior people misapplying them. Second, there must be a means of shaping or correcting the institutional behaviour before it takes hold. In both cases, the implementation of the CDS' Principles had its challenges and the subject warrants a closer examination.

SUCCESSION PLANNING

Early in his tenure, General Hillier saw the need to address succession planning in a very practical way. He believed, as did others, that the merit system had become too formula-driven and not enough judgement was being applied. Too often, the result was that officers who looked good on paper did not measure up in practice. This was particularly a concern at executive levels where the CF needed to select not only good leaders but people suited to fill a range of demanding senior positions. This meant that G/FOs had to be well suited for their jobs and sufficiently versatile to fill a number of demanding positions. Unfortunately, such was not the case and General Hillier faced a situation in which he was limited as to where he could employ senior officers.

General Hillier started the process of changing the executive merit system and shaping the G/FO corps to support the achievement of his vision for the CF. Indeed, the last two years have seen a considerable number of senior officers retire, a number of them in advance of that required. In addition, the demography and complexion of the G/FO corps has fundamentally changed.

There has been some intimation within the CF that such action is inappropriate. However, such is not necessarily the case. A change leader must shape the organization as he sees best, considering the needs of the institution and the quality of the pool from which he has to choose leaders. The example of industry and business, where executive leaders' fortunes change quickly depending on their accomplishments, should be borne in mind. The CF requires the best leadership that the country has to offer and the CDS should take a no less direct approach to ensuring that reality. G/FOs should understand always that they serve at the pleasure of the CDS.

Understandably, any change to the merit system, in particular such an approach as described, creates friction amongst the senior leadership. To be effective, to ensure fairness and to maintain trust in the system, such decision-making must be, to the greatest extent possible, collaborative amongst the senior leadership and transparent in its approach. But, in the final analysis, the CDS must choose those leaders that he believes best meet the needs of the CF.

As stated earlier, the timing and selection of the CDS' replacement would be a key factor in managing the change initiative, and one must presume that General Hillier gave some thought to his replacement and the implications of who might be selected. However, given that the choice is made by the PM on the recommendation of the MND, General Hillier's ability to influence such selection is limited at best. As with all order-in-council appointments, the CDS serves at the pleasure of the PM. Accordingly, it was unclear how long General Hillier would remain in his position until the formal announcement of his retirement, effective 1 July 2008.

Given the short-term pressures on the CDS, little effort has been focused on the long term. With the restructuring of NDHQ as of 2007-2008, the principal focus has been on the redesign of the whole Force Development process and structure. As a consequence, there has been little if any real work on the next phases of development. Given the load that the CF is carrying and the limited capacity from which they must draw, this is understandable. Indeed, the reality is that change requires making some priorities and parking certain requirements until later. The one danger here is to allow such deferment to carry on too long.

SUMMARY

Facing a high operational tempo and the demands of ongoing change, General Hillier had to limit what he could achieve in shaping the institution for the long term. His expectation was that the articulation of his broad principles would form his statement of intent and guide many to do the right thing to achieve the kind of CF he envisaged. Where he did focus was on people and he put considerable effort into shaping the CF leadership for the long term. In this regard, there can be no doubt that he has been successful. The leadership of today's CF is a reflection of General Hillier's influence and expectations for the institution – a leadership that will shape the CF for many years to come.

CHAPTER 9

ASSESSMENT AND LESSONS LEARNED

Having looked at the details and specifics of change through this period, it is now time to stand back and look at the broad aspect of CF Transformation in order to understand the critical factors in its evolution and to make some assessment of what it has meant for the CF.

TRANSFORMATION – THE WISDOM OF CHANGE

Change is a demanding dynamic for any leader or organization and is not something that should be entered into lightly. Indeed, looking back over the past three years, many within the institution are asking the question, "Was it wise to commence such an undertaking?" Such "arm chair quarterbacking" is understandable given all that the DND/CF is now facing in its uncertain future. However, such questions do need to be asked.

There is little doubt that, in the early part of this century, the CF was facing major challenges that called into question its long-term viability and value to the nation. This is a harsh statement, and is not meant to imply that this small military was not a quality organization. In addition, there is no doubt that, compared to the previous 15 years, things were clearly "looking up". However, any knowledgeable analyst must question whether continuation of the CF's hand-to-mouth existence, trying to maintain the same scope and level of capability, would really meet the needs of the nation in the 21st century.

Clearly, General Hillier did not believe the *status quo* was either sustainable or viable for Canada. When he was given an opportunity to change it, he had to decide, with very little time to assess all of the factors, whether he would take the risk, inherent in the fast-paced approach to change, that he knew would be required. There is little doubt that his decisions to take the job as CDS and to transform the institution were taken together. Not by nature one to be a "caretaker", General Hillier came into the position because he felt strongly that the change was required. In his view, the risks were acceptable because the objective was so important.

TRANSFORMATION – THE WISDOM OF APPROACH

Some will argue that the time was not right, that the lack of clear resourcing and the certainty that operations in Afghanistan would take their toll on the CF, should have predicated a delay in organizational change, or at least a more measured approach. As one commentator argued, the approach was misguided as the resources did not exist to achieve the ends; like departing on a 1000 km journey with only 800 km of fuel.

However, the perspective of the CDS was that at no time would conditions be right for such levels of change. To delay or slow down would only sacrifice the opportunity provided. Indeed, change within the CF was an essential element of the strategy to set the conditions for achieving the long-term goal. For only by establishing the institution's credibility, and demonstrating the value that it could have for meeting the nation's interests, would the necessary support and resources be forthcoming. The strategy adopted was rightly one that best fit General Hillier's personal style and abilities. He is by nature an intuitive, strategic thinker and he saw the broad thrusts he would have to make to create the change required. He is also by training and experience an operational leader, so he naturally tended to see much through an operations prism. This not only coloured his view on what change was required, but very much shaped his thinking in terms of how it was best accomplished. But, what has been accomplished over these years of CF Transformation and how has the change gone?

An inspiring vision delivered with passion by a charismatic leader. CF Transformation was launched with vigour and very much captured the imagination of most observers, both within the CF and across the nation. General Hillier's vision, delivered with passion and conviction resonated with many and, if the substance of the message was lacking at times, the energy definitely was not. Perhaps most importantly, this was a military leader who had presence, a "soldier's soldier", and many were inspired and re-energized by him. The troops felt that, finally, here was a leader to lead them out of the wilderness! For Canadians used to political leaders coloured in shades of grey, here was a colourful, charismatic leader to brighten their mood and to make them feel good about themselves at a time when they needed it most.

The challenge of getting the team on board. By far, one of the most important and difficult tasks for the change leader is that of developing the team, getting all on board with his vision and strategy, and keeping them engaged. There is little doubt that most were inspired by the vision and the style of this new CDS, and all looked forward with anticipation to the new world he promised. However, some of the more senior and experienced officers, those who understood well the limits that the institution was facing, had their doubts. In the final analysis, the degree of unity achieved was a direct result of the ability to achieve a shared vision and a level of trust between the CDS and his leaders.

Shared vision. The vision was captivating but never fully understood, and it certainly was not shared by all of the leadership. This was caused primarily by concerns over achievability and inclusiveness, which resulted in a fragmented vision and approach to achieving it.

Unquestionably, the vision was inspiring, and many saw it as a new and better world that all could sign on to. However, the CDS had not operationalized it, that is to say, defined the details of the process, with the result that it was not clear. Given the lack of time to conduct planning before launching transformation, this lack of clarity on the end state was understandable. But, with the passage of time, the problems were still not resolved. The vision became no clearer. In part, this was due to the inability to resolve the resource and capability issues and get a strategic plan approved. However, it was also driven by changing circumstances or decisions, such as the responsibility for force generation or the approval of the SCTF. The result of this uncertainty was to cast doubt on the viability of the vision and, certainly, to call into question the impact of its implementation on all players. Indeed, at the CDS' Seminar in May of 2007, this lack of specificity of the vision was one of the key concerns of the G/FOs. In this regard, there were two key problems to achieving a shared vision.

First, there was the problem of inclusiveness. Many could not see themselves within the vision or, if so, in a much-reduced role. The navy and air force were particularly concerned over what some saw as an army-centric vision that they perceived as minimizing their role to one of support. Perhaps, more significant was the lack of assurances that the resources would be there to ensure the maintenance of the kind of combat capability the environments believed they needed to fulfill their roles. There was also a concern on the part of all ECS over their roles in the evolving DND/CF structure. The creation of the operational level command structure would, at a minimum, see a shift in power within the CF that, unquestionably, caused concern in many quarters. Moreover, an initial recommendation from CAT 1 had been that all force generation would come under Commander of Canada Command and that the ECS would become two-star level advisers to the CDS. This proposal had enraged the ECS as they saw this as an illogical move that belied the importance of force generation. This recommendation was never implemented and, indeed it is not clear how seriously the recommendation was considered by the CDS. Still, it remained an issue of uncertainty and a source of friction for a long time, and as a consequence, the embracing of the vision by many of the senior leaders remained, at best, lukewarm.

Second, there persisted a genuine concern over the ability to achieve the vision as originally stated in 2005. Part of this worry came from the belief that the resources were not sufficient – and would not become sufficient – to achieve all that the CDS envisaged. Part of it was skepticism, at times bordering on cynicism, that the institution would be able to make the adjustments required and, if achieved, whether they could be sustained. Both of these issues had their genesis in bitter experience. The resource challenge was not a new problem and all of the leadership had been through the massive cuts of the 1990s, with their accompanying belt tightening efficiencies, and had genuine doubts that the existing capability structure was sustainable. This was particularly so with respect to the major capital fleets that would need to be replaced and for which adequate funding was unavailable. The vision also included the demands for more people for new structures or capability, the availability of which many questioned. Some, such as the army, had a particular concern, as it saw the creation of Special Operations Forces Command as a fourth environment, a proposal too rich to sustain and that would ultimately denude the army's ability to generate the land force required.

Additionally, as organizational changes got underway with the new command and control structure, grave concerns were expressed over the ability to stretch the limited number of people over what would become a larger organization. These concerns of senior officers and other members partly came from previous experiences with restructuring, one well-known example being the MCCRT. It had included attempts to introduce a variety of novel approaches for running DND, to incorporate a less centralized philosophy, and to generate a more innovative culture that would permit the maintenance of a very lean, but still effective, C2 structure. The result on this occasion was a great deal of turmoil and, ultimately, no substantive change to the organization other than a massive cut in personnel. The result was fewer people attempting to do more.

However, the problem was not only achievability of the vision; it also included problems of inclusiveness in the transformation process. Driven in part by the need to develop the vision early, the CDS relied largely on a small staff and some trusted advisers to shape the way ahead. For whatever reason, he did not take the ECS into his confidence for some time and they, for all practical purposes, did not play a major role in shaping the vision. As a consequence, the leadership did not come together early enough in the process and this created a sense that ECS were not trusted. A number of senior leaders were skeptical from the beginning and vocal in their concerns that resulted in them being seen as resistant to change. This set the tone for much of the dynamic with the result that many did not enthusiastically embrace the vision and took a wait-and-see attitude.

General Hillier understood the concerns over lack of inclusion. After all, the debate had raged for 40 years about the respective roles in the CF and who had which capabilities! He probably felt, however, that the matter could be overcome once people saw the opportunity the vision would create. His view was that this vision was based in large measure on a rational view of the world in a post-9/11 era, and on a pragmatic approach to ensuring Canada has influence within it. He believed that this would portend great opportunity for the CF and lead to a resolution of many of the problems he saw within the existing structure and culture. It is likely that he did not fully expect the degree of concern expressed by some of the key players.

In a similar way, the achievability issue was not a surprise, as all parts of the CF had been living a marginal existence for some time. The CDS saw the implementation of a new CF vision as an opportunity to resolve many of the shortfalls facing the CF, which by showing a willingness to change and truly embracing reform, all would gain. He was a risk taker and did not appreciate the degree of risk aversion that others would have. Could this have been overcome if the key players, in particular the ECS, had been included more fully in the initial discussions and vision shaping? It is possible, although one cannot say with certainty. It is unclear why the ECS did not play a greater role in the early stages, although the need for speed was clearly a dominant factor. However, while not a fatal decision, it tended to marginalize the roles of the ECS, and it did indicate that the CDS was not sufficiently sensitive to the needs of the environments and the future consequences.

ACHIEVING UNITY

Few amongst the leadership of the CF would not intuitively understand the importance of unity to achieving CF Transformation. This is not just the sharing of the vision, but having unity of thought in terms of how the change was to be achieved, unity of purpose in terms of the specifics of the end state being pursued, and unity of action in terms of the specific actions and priorities that need to be undertaken. To achieve this level of unity, all have to be in the mind of the change leader, such that they can make decisions on the many changes required, in line with his philosophy and intent, without reference to him. In due course, this level of unity needs to permeate the whole institution, for over time it becomes the essence of the institutional doctrine and organizational culture for the transformed CF.

The degree of unity within the CF, and particularly amongst the senior leadership, was unclear. There is little doubt that all worked hard to implement the many changes directed and, equally, that they genuinely wanted to achieve the best possible results. Indeed, there is no question that these leaders were professional in their actions and loyal in their intent. But, that did not mean that they saw the issues similarly or acted in a united manner.

Achieving such unity must start at the top. It literally requires being in someone else's mind and imposes on the change leader the requirement to commit the time and effort required to allow this to happen. This is neither quick nor easy to achieve. It requires the willingness to discuss, even debate, the various aspects of what the institution is trying to achieve and how it must achieve it. The change leader must be prepared to explain in some detail his views and persuade his subordinates of the wisdom of his approach. Equally, he needs to be prepared to be convinced of better approaches and ultimately to have the self-confidence to agree to change his approach based on superior ideas, or to achieve greater unity. This process not only enhances understanding, but it builds mutual trust and credibility in the change strategy and plan. As the strategy and various change plans are developed and implemented, this dynamic of building unity must continue and at no time can it be taken for granted.

The unity amongst the senior leadership of the CF throughout this period was variable. With many changes in substance and approach, and as people transferred and issues changed, the degree of unity waxed and waned. The overall degree of unity was never as high as one would desire to sustain such an ambitious program as CF Transformation. The reasons are many.

The command relationship between the CDS and his G/FOs was at times one of conflict. As with all such relationships, there were many reasons, factors and personalities involved. Indeed, this is a very difficult and sensitive subject to address, and there is a danger in over-generalizing and misrepresenting the true chemistry in a very challenging and dynamic situation. However, some degree of understanding of the situation is essential for future leaders.

The first and arguably most influential aspect of the command relationship was the CDS' leadership style. General Hillier approached his role as CDS in a similar manner to that of an operational commander. In part, this was due to his background and experience, principally as an operational commander. However, his approach was also the consequence of a conscious decision as he believed it was just this aspect of command that the DND/CF corporate culture needed to change. Following this operational model, he anticipated that he would make clear his intent, he would seek the views and advice of his subordinates, and then he would decide how the CF would proceed. He was comfortable with others discussing or even debating the elements of the emerging plan, but did not see himself engaging in that debate. He saw in the interminable corporate debates so familiar in NDHQ the source of much confusion, lack of direction and loss of valuable time and energy. This was part of the culture he intended to change.

However, this approach, in a consensus culture quite used to such debates, did not help his cause. His senior leaders, especially the ECS responsible as they were to preserve the environments' operational capability, were seriously concerned over the potential consequences of the changes planned. They needed and wanted the time and opportunity to debate the various elements of the change plan, to genuinely understand where they were going and, as necessary, to convince the CDS of essential changes. While some of this, as earlier described, related to issues of achieving a shared vision, the core of this was building trust. The CDS listened to concerns and issues from ECS and others but tended not to debate them. In his view, he took into account that which he needed to, in order to make his decisions. This dynamic created an environment that set the stage for some difficulties in command relationships. The situation was exacerbated by certain other issues that eroded mutual trust.

The future of the ECS and who would be responsible for force generation was a key concern. The proposal that Canada Command would be responsible for force generation, and that the ECS would be reduced to two-star advisors was, in the view of the ECS, a great backward step. They were of the view that the environments' ability to generate force had been the saving grace in a military that had seen great erosion of capability. To hand this over to one commander, who would not necessarily understand the important environmental dynamics, was foolhardy. Despite expressing these concerns, they could not get clarity on their roles or future. There was also a sense that the real vision was for a large army and a small navy and air force, that this CDS was using his time to parochially advance his own vision. The letter General Hillier had signed as CLS in 2003 came back to haunt him.

Beyond the organizational dynamic, there were serious issues raised with respect to the CDS' treatment of his G/FOs. As part of his plans to reform the succession planning process, the CF saw a significant loss on retirement of G/FOs. Some of this was natural and part of the normal demographics, but some was clearly a result of the CDS shaping the G/FO corps for the future. This created a sense of lack of respect that was exacerbated by some ill-chosen words made by the CDS on the need of the institution to move certain officers on. This was further complicated by the promotion and appointment of a number of army generals into key positions that raised the spectre of nepotism. In some respects, the final straw was the announcement, at a time when the senior leadership was under great stress, of a reduction in the total number of generals, flag officers and colonels/captains(navy). The result of this was a general sense that the CDS did not value them and that he was shaping the institution to meet his personal desires.

In the final analysis, the dynamic in which the CF found itself was understandable and, given the personalities involved, difficult to resolve. The CDS saw some of his G/FOs as resistant to change and unwilling to take risks, or even to compromise, in pursuit of strategic objectives he genuinely felt were critical to the future of the CF. He also saw the need to reshape the senior officer corps to better meet the needs of the CF in the 21st century. However, some of his subordinates saw a CDS who did not listen to their concerns, who apparently did not understand or care about the risks to the institution, and who did not take their advice. The result was an erosion of mutual respect and trust.

CREDIBILITY

While the unity amongst the senior leadership may not have been as strong as one would wish, it is not the only factor in advancing the change initiative. As the change leader, General Hillier was the visionary and CF Transformation was his initiative. How people saw him very much reflected their sense of Transformation. This was so much so that virtually all activities came to be seen to some degree as transformative, whether they were or not. While the senior leadership closest to the change issues had their own concerns with the CDS' plans for transformation, many both internal and external to the CF had different and influential views. In the final analysis, the CDS' credibility with Canadians and the members of the CF provided a strong counter balance to any lack of unity amongst the senior leadership.

General Hillier has become a public persona like no CDS before him. In a country largely devoid of strong public leaders on the national stage, he stood out as a rare figure; strong, direct and open, committed to the nation and the military, focused on serving his troops and helping those in need. Even more significant, he is a very human person, with a folksy style and self-deprecating humour that endears him to many. In short, he is a charismatic leader of integrity – a true servant of the people. That this should be the reality for a military leader in such an unmilitary nation is truly remarkable and even his greatest detractors will admit that, from this perspective alone, General Hillier proved to be a tremendous benefit to the CF.

All military personnel want leadership. They want someone to tell them what is happening, to affirm their mission or task, and to make sense of the complex environment in which they live. They want someone who is there to share the trials, tribulations and risks with them, someone who is there to laugh and to cry with them. General Hillier has been all of this and more. Significantly, he has overseen the conduct of the highest level of operations and has, through focusing the institution on operations, ensured an unparalleled level of support to the people in the front line. It should be no surprise, then, that the trust amongst the fighting troops, and credibility with environmental personnel in the field, was very high. Indeed, the closer to the lower ranks of the CF, the greater the loyalty to the CDS. It is instructive that when media reports in the fall of 2007 indicated that General Hillier might be replaced, there was a public outcry from some of the troops, a situation almost unheard of in the past, and a sharp contrast with the mid-1990s.

Much of this view is shared by the senior leadership of the CF, the issues of unity and trust notwithstanding. All are most impressed with what has been accomplished in the operational context and the raising of the status of the CF in the nation. It is well recognized that General Hillier has achieved great things for the military. However, that credibility is counter-balanced to a large degree by concerns over the cost of such gains. There are genuine worries about the sustainability of the tempo of operations and, given the absolute top priority afforded operations, the consequences on other parts of the CF. Some people are asking whether the price is too high.

Interestingly, the external perspective closely parallels the internal one. Much as with the troops in the front lines, the Canadian public is largely impressed with General Hillier and see him as truly the face of the CF. However, equally, there are doubts about his approach and the conse-quences of his actions. Politically, there is clearly discomfort with a general with such a strong public persona, and the replacement of Gordon O'Connor as MND, given the conflict with the CDS, is a good indication of the strength of the CDS' public credibility.

Given the degree of shared vision and unity amongst the senior leadership, one might question whether Transformation could be successful. However, General Hillier's personal credibility counts for much in this dynamic and it allowed him to accomplish a great deal. The key factor in his ability to realize his vision would be his ability to solidify the gains made and create a new foundation while he remained CDS.

Maintaining organizational coherence during change. Running any organization during a period of major change, especially large and complex organizations, requires careful attention to the essentials of management. Leadership is by far the most vital component of effecting change within an organization. However, while both are required to be effective, management speaks to the requirements for organizational coherence. The importance is high for effective planning, organizing, directing and controlling of the organization, in line with the leadership strategy, to jointly meet the stated objectives. If the management of the "corporation" does not fulfill these functions effectively, no amount of leadership will solve the problem.

In order to ensure all parts of the organization understand the changes being made and can adapt to them, the leadership at all levels must understand clearly what changes or activities are intended and their particular roles in them. This requires an understanding of the decisions being made, and clear direction on the actions that all leaders must take. It is also vital that there are regular communications throughout the organization as to what change has occurred and the results of it. Only in this way can all maintain an understanding of the many elements of change within the institution.

Planning and ensuring coherence. As has been addressed earlier, the development of internal plans is vital to the understanding and coordinating of the change intended. This was not a strength during this period. While the vision was the focus, the CDS did not espouse a clear strategy for getting there, and no such strategic document was ever written. The result was that, while all had their view of how Transformation was to unfold and the broad thrusts envisaged, these tended to be individual perspectives as opposed to a shared or common view. The result was that the "commander's intent" so strongly held by the CDS in his mission command philosophy was not always clear.

This limitation of the strategic approach was exacerbated by the lack of more detailed planning that could have ensured that the specific goals and the actions required were better understood. The lack of a published road map, campaign plan or "master implementation plan", even as a document to guide internal activities, had serious consequences for not only the senior leadership but the institution. The result was a senior leadership expected to act in a mission command sense, but without clarity on what they were trying to achieve or how they were supposed to get there. The effect was that they didn't provide the type of guidance required by the many staffs in the organization. These staffs, still operating very much on the "matrix" model, lacked clear coherent direction and had no plan with which to work. This meant that, at best, they made it up as they went along; at worst, they did nothing.

Part of the problem faced here was due to the lack of capacity and continuity of staffs focused on planning for and managing change. Whether by design, or as a result of other pressures, the CF achieved an unfortunate degree of organizational disruption with respect to the planning for and management of change. The CATs were organized quickly, were not particularly well coordinated in their efforts, and then were disbanded with minimum time to stand up the CFTT that in turn was dissolved soon after it reached full stride. Responsibility for managing change then fell to the VCDS' new CFD and CProg organizations that had a limited capacity to achieve all that was required. The result of this turmoil was a fracturing of the coherence essential to good organizational management. While much was done and major disconnects were avoided, this was more as a result of the hard work of a few key players.

MANAGING CHANGE – MATCHING CAPACITY AND AMBITION

The old saying that "A man's reach must exceed his grasp" is a sound personal philosophy but it has serious implications for an organization undergoing change. To maintain organizational effectiveness and cohesion, the level of ambition must be carefully balanced with the capacity of the institution to implement and coordinate the actions required. Unquestionably, General Hillier's expectations for change during his tenure were very high and he intentionally pushed the organization to do as much as he thought it could. However, there is some evidence that capacity is a continuing problem that has and will continue to impact the CF's attempts to change.

The capacity is related to two aspects of the problem. First is the ability of the organization to physically restructure. It must be recognized that creating new organizations requires people to be extracted from existing organizations, so the whole institution is affected. Second is the organization's ability to manage and coordinate all that is going on. The more activities or tasks the organizations are required to undertake, and specifically the amount of change that is occurring, are very much limited by the size, quality and effectiveness of the staffs.

In the context of CF Transformation, there have been two major examples of this issue. The stand up of four new operational command headquarters demanded a large number of experienced staff, which created a major strain on the institution as the requisite staffs had to be extracted from elsewhere in the structure. The creation of the Special Operations Forces (SOF) capability also saw the recruiting of a significant number of the best quality personnel from the three environments, in particular the army, at a time when the operational tempo was high.

Balancing ambition with capacity is always a challenge and, unquestionably, it is a major concern within the CF. Two aspects added significantly to the degree of difficulty. First was the increase in the tempo of operations. It was not just the number of troops, but the change in intensity that had the greatest consequences. From the beginning, the CDS had made clear that operations came first and that the CF would have no higher priority. With the move of the Canadian contingent in Afghanistan from Kabul to the Kandahar region, and in particular as casualties mounted, the strain on the whole structure increased significantly. Support to operations consumed a greater and greater part of the CF's energy, particularly at the strategic level, as the organization worked overtime to improve the survivability of the troops in contact, while appropriately managing the consequences of the casualties. Second, with the change in government, a great amount of energy was consumed to respond to the political change in direction. This was not only a matter of harmonizing visions but especially accelerating initiatives, such as new capital projects that the government wished to advance.

The consequence of all this was a CF that was overloaded and, with the benefit of hindsight, seemingly lacked the ability to make the really tough choices. The reality is that during a period of change, it is vital that the institution carefully balance its level of ambition with its capacity. If it does not, it risks failing in all areas and thereby accomplishing nothing. In this case, the CF has managed to "keep its head above water" through a very difficult period. However, it has come at a price. There is a limit to how long people can focus on achieving everything by "heroic effort", and the clock is running!

Maintaining common purpose and intent. Through a period of intense change, it is vital that the senior leadership in particular maintains a clear understanding of the state of change and a clear commonality of purpose and intent. This implies not only good communications on actions taken, but involvement in and understanding of the many decisions and adjustments that must occur as the leadership balances conflicting requirements. Here again, there is some doubt that the CF maintained a good degree of common understanding.

On the communications front, the record is not good. Over the years of CF Transformation, there have been a total of five Transformation SITREPs, the sum total of the official written communications on the subject. While there have clearly been many more opportunities to ensure people understand the state of change, e.g., articles in the *Maple Leaf* magazine, the publishing of these SITREPS is indicative of the general trend and approach to Transformation. The first four were evenly spaced between mid-2005 and mid-2006, clearly the period of most significant Transformation activity. However, the final one was not published until September 2007 and there has been nothing since then.

The problem for the leadership, though, is not just having broad situational updates. Rather, they need more detailed understanding of what is happening and why. The issue is one largely of change governance, as the senior leadership needs to be genuinely involved in all that is happening. Initially, this worked reasonably well and the CDS held close to ten AFCs, twice the regular number, in the February-June 2005 timeframe, largely focused in the change initiative. However, this focus waned over time.

The specific governance structure established by CT appears not to have been a major factor in the decision-making process. Driven as much by the "command centric" philosophy, transformation issues tended to be identified by CFTT staff, which CT would then take to the CDS for decision. Consultation was not the norm with the consequence that the senior leadership was not always aware of the decisions being taken and did not feel part of that process. Indeed, it is apparent that commanders would often discuss their plans with the CDS privately and receive direction or approval without full consideration of the institutional consequences. In such a circumstance, maintenance of common purpose and intent is difficult, if not impossible.

Leading the institution during change. General Hillier's personal influence has been the principal driving force behind Transformation, and his ability as a charismatic leader and communicator has been the foundation of this credibility. The result, both internally and externally, has been profound, bringing the CF front and centre in the national consciousness. Canadians who only a few years before knew nothing of the CF and what it did were suddenly embracing our men and women in uniform, wearing red on Fridays, and sporting "support our troops" stickers on their vehicles. This higher public profile and the support that came with it, combined with a greater, more effective operational involvement, resulted in much higher morale and sense of self-worth within the CF. For the majority of the CF and for the Canadian public, this was all a result of the leadership of General Hillier, and he could do no wrong.

Government support and credibility is much more difficult to gauge. In general, governments do not like generals who are politically active and potentially unpredictable. However, despite media reports to the contrary, there has been no clear indication of a lack of government support for the CDS. And, even if there were, the level of public support is a reasonable counterweight.

As is his custom, General Hillier led CF Transformation from the front. He was the face of change within the CF and his effect was motivational, particularly with respect to the troops and the public. Accordingly, it was here that he concentrated his effort, perhaps realizing that his ability to influence all aspects of the institution, in particular to achieve great gains with his principal subordinates, was limited. Arguably, by maintaining a broad level of support, his overall credibility remained high, providing him the influence and flexibility he required to sustain transformation.

SUMMARY

The demands of organizational change are considerable, more so for military organizations, and require the change leader to maintain the energy for the change initiative, and to manage the perceptions and expectations of many stakeholders and constituencies, all while maintaining institutional stability and balance. General Hillier understood these requirements extremely well and, while his ability to adhere to them was limited, it was not from lack of effort. He is a strategic leader and clearly had the long-term vision in his mind at all times. Unfortunately, events, some beyond his control, detracted him from ensuring that the management of change was properly focused. As a result, over time, the energy for Transformation waned. As with any organization, operations are primary. Without sustaining operations, the organization fails. In this Transformation, the extremely high tempo of operations in 2006 and 2007 placed great pressure on the CDS that had a clear effect on his ability to maintain the momentum of change.

CHAPTER 10

CONCLUSIONS AND FUTURE CHALLENGES

Attempting to provide an overall assessment of CF Transformation is far from easy. It is, after all, a process still in progress, and there is much more to be done before anyone can conclude with certainty that it has achieved its intended purpose. However, it is a superb case study of an institutional leader leading change. This is not to suggest that General Hillier as the change leader either did everything right or wrong. Rather it shows a strong, visionary leader making reasoned judgments as he shaped the change process and the institution to his will. In so doing, he achieved considerable success, but not without difficulty or setback.

General Hillier was provided an opportunity that few Chiefs of the Defence Staff have ever received. He was approached by a government that wanted the CF to become more effective, was willing to provide the resources required, and was prepared to provide him a relatively free hand. Given his firm belief that the CF needed to change, he seized upon the opportunity given him. Unquestionably, he had doubts and concerns but he is by nature a risk taker and felt the risks manageable.

In launching CF Transformation, General Hillier took a sound strategic approach. Realizing that he had limited time available to prepare, he eschewed detailed plans in favour of a dynamic, command-led strategy. Relying on his own experience and playing to his own strengths, he developed a strategy intentionally focused to unseat the existing culture and create a more malleable environment. By creating a new command structure and moving the operational focus out of NDHQ, he fractured the existing staff-centric bureaucracy. Then, by emphasizing the effectiveness of operations, he shifted the balance away from staff processes and reshaped C2 to drive change to DND and CF culture.

Perhaps the most significant factor in his approach was his personal charismatic style. In presenting his vision and selling himself to the members of the CF and the Canadian public, he established a solid foundation of understanding and trust. This credibility provided him with the essential support both within and outside the institution – support that became the foundation upon which his Transformation efforts were built.

General Hillier believed that speed was vital in creating the conditions for change, and shaped his strategy accordingly. Some observers will argue that time was not that critical and will suggest that more planning would have overcome many of the problems he encountered. However, he made a sound decision to proceed quickly, given his overall objective, but one that was to haunt him throughout the change process.

The CDS was not able to achieve the level of unity or consensus that he would have preferred. To some degree, this was driven by factors beyond his control, as he could not promise the CF leadership that which he could not deliver. There also was some criticism that he did not invest the requisite time and effort building greater understanding, or was not as open to compromise as he should have been to achieve a shared vision. There may be some merit in that view, but it is likely that the CDS saw this increasingly as too high an investment for the probable return. In the final analysis, he was prepared to work around people, if necessary, relying instead on the great support of the members of the CF and the public to sustain him.

General Hillier's strategy was founded on his personal experience and philosophy and, as an armour officer, he took a manoeuvrist approach to the problem. He saw the need to overcome institutional inertia, not unlike that of attacking a defensive position, and his strategy, much like the German Blitzkrieg, was intended to break through and destabilize the situation. He could then consolidate the gains, mop up, and prepare to attack again. While clearly understanding the need to plan such a strategy, he saw detailed planning as wasteful of time and, potentially, as jeopardizing attainment of his objective.

The rapid implementation of a new CF command and control structure was very much General Hillier's Blitzkrieg, disrupting the old NDHQ matrix structure and culture while ensuring that he and his operational commanders retained the initiative. Unquestionably, this action created the environment he sought – an environment of constructive chaos – and the new structure was in place in a remarkably short time. But, this action was not without consequences as the organization that he had disrupted was equally essential to realizing his aims. After all, the corporate structure was the firm foundation upon which the CF operated, and it had also been seriously affected by change and loss of capacity. Added to this the lack of detailed planning created some uncertainty and even constipation in moving forward on essential issues.

While this risk was acceptable to him in order to achieve the aim, it was less so as time passed. The CF corporate structure was, as a result of the change, fragile and lacking requisite capacity. This exacerbated the impact of a lack of detailed planning and contributed to erosion in cohesion. Much of this has been recognized, but completing these plans and realigning all elements of the institution now will take time. Indeed, it has been recognized, at a number of levels, that additional changes, essential to improve the overall effectiveness and efficiency of the institution, will have to wait until the tempo is somewhat reduced.

Consideration of the results of CF Transformation must take into account the changing events during its implementation. As with any journey, there are always bumps in the road and, certainly, General Hillier encountered them. Perhaps the most difficult period came with the arrival of a new government. As with any such change, harmonizing ongoing initiatives with the new government agenda was expected to take time, and there was always the potential for directed change to plans. However, the very different visions of the CF, held by the new MND and the CDS, created considerable tension and resulted in an inordinate amount of time passing before an agreed upon way forward was reached. The effects of this were to both slow and alter the CDS' plans for Transformation. Most significantly, it resulted in a shift of the ground under the CDS. He had started Transformation with the full and committed support of the government and had proceeded on that basis. Then, having launched this high risk venture, his political support was, at best, eroding.

Simultaneous with the arrival of the new government, the operational situation in Afghanistan heated up. Having moved to the Kandahar region, the CF's Task Force Afghanistan now was undertaking major combat operations and, significantly, taking casualties. The effect of this was to increase the demands on the CF, its leadership, and the government in managing the conflict, which in turn, added considerable pressure to all activities of the CF.

The secondary consequence of these challenges, given the reduction in available time, capacity and political support, was most certainly to slow down the change initiative. In some cases, such as the government decision to suspend the SCTF, the specific plans had to be adjusted in order to achieve the objectives. However, whether these will have a long-term effect is difficult to gauge.

Whether by design or as a result of the delays created by these challenges, the CF Transformation now, in the 2008-2009 period, is in a consolidation phase. Much of this is building on the work done by "the three wise men" in their reports.[54] The real test will be whether, following the considerable delay, the next CDS can re-energize his Transformation efforts.

THE FUTURE OF TRANSFORMATION

In spite of the challenges faced, there can be no question that General Hillier has created significant change within the CF. He has put in place a new command and control structure that is fundamentally changing the way in which the CF and DND operate. In addition, he has created a dynamic that has already shaped a much more operationally focused organization. He started a shift in institutional culture to meet these demands. The organization is arguably already much more agile.

But, there remain doubts. There are concerns as to the sustainability of the command and control structure over the long term. There are questions as to whether the evolving shape of the CF will meet the defence needs of the country. Perhaps the greatest issue of all remains the continuing challenge of shaping the CF culture, one focused on operations. Such hand-wringing will always be present, supported by those who would maintain the *status quo*. While it is easy to focus on the risks and the failures, one should reflect on the positive changes and the potential that the future holds.

Change is not a destination but a journey. The implementation of CF Transformation has laid a foundation and created a dynamic that should see the institution continue to adapt. The ultimate impact of this change will depend in part on how well the CDS has been able to consolidate his efforts and to firm up that foundation. But, ultimately, it will depend on his successors.

It is said that changing an organization that has seen a long period of relative stability is much like moving a large rock in a garden. The greatest challenge is getting it out of the mud, so that it can be moved. Thereafter, moving it anywhere can be relatively easy. One may debate whether General Hillier has been able to get the rock moving, but there is no doubt that he has unleashed the suction around it and turned it over. Movement now is inevitable.

ANNEX A

CHIEF OF THE DEFENCE STAFF
TRANSFORMATION PRINCIPLES – AN ANALYSIS

The CDS published his transformation principles in his CDS SITREP 02/05 in September 2005. In so doing, he stated that the principles:

...are intended to guide commanders and staffs as they execute transformation activities. They are not dogmatic and no principle supersedes another. Judgment must be exercised in their use however they articulate a perspective that should routinely inform on-going analysis and decision-making. In the longer term, these principles will help re-shape and renew CF culture, creating a shared ethos fundamental to the creation of a CF that is relevant, responsive and effective in an increasingly unstable and volatile strategic environment.

The following reflects the principles and definitions as published, followed by an analysis.

Canadian Forces Identity. *Our first loyalty is to Canada. Beyond this fundamental imperative, all service personnel must look past environment, component or unit affiliations to most closely identify with the CF. The greater good of Canada and the CF will, in every instance, take precedence over considerations of service, component or unit affiliation.*

This principle entreated members of the CF to focus on the higher loyalty to the nation and the CF. It was clearly aimed to address the matter of environmental parochialism. It is valid as a statement of philosophy and an essential first principle to achieve the kind of integrated culture the CDS sought. However, the statement by itself is unlikely to address the underlying issues.

In applying this principle, one must consider it in two contexts. First, in an operational context, the CDS was concerned about the need for environments to work together in an integrated or joint sense. Here, given the general focus of mission first, which all environments adopted, true jointness should realistically be easy to achieve. But, the problem is one of common understanding, as each of the environments had developed its own culture and doctrine, or interpretation of doctrine, such that they could not integrate easily. The CDS' intent to get the environments to work together in an integrated fashion, to learn together, clearly was the right approach. Achieving success here required far more than a simple statement of the principle and, thus, the CDS approach to joint command and control.

The second context is the effectiveness of the culture in a corporate environment. Here, the challenge is for the senior leadership, in particular the environmental chiefs, to develop an integrated strategy to meet the defence and security needs of the nation. The problem is how and where to compromise to achieve the best possible capability for the resources available.

On the surface, this may seem to an observer to be an easy problem, but it is not. Traditionally the issue is presented as the environments fighting for dominance, that is, to have a bigger navy, army or air force and to see the world and Canada's defence requirements through the parochial prism of that environment. But, historically, abundance and growth have not been a Canadian military problem. So, at its root, the question is not what we do build, as it is always easy to grow, but rather with what do we do away. In short, if the resources do not exist, can we not just do away with some capability, and accept the risk, while still achieving a requisite level of capability.

The challenge then is to develop a strategy that truly ensures an effective level of defence, by accepting risk through the elimination of some capabilities. In short, how do we defend the country having cut a major part, or perhaps all, of one of the environments? And, if that is objectively achievable, how do we ensure that all those, affected by these cuts from the environments, accept such a reduction? As Douglas L. Bland stated in his book, *Chiefs of Defence*, a CDS "must be possessed of a higher loyalty" to make such tough decisions for the good of the country.[55] However, it is almost certainly unrealistic to expect that one can generate a complete professional culture able to do likewise. The statement of this principle makes this aspect of the challenge no easier. Indeed, it can be argued that an environmental chief resisting the decimation of his environment by what he sees as a misguided CDS is being loyal to the country.

Command Centric Imperative. *The CF command and control structure must be optimized to provide the most effective and responsive decision and operational support to designated strategic, operational and tactical commanders. This principle imposes the requirement to clearly delineate and separate line and staff functions, establishing a distinct and unambiguous chain of command that coherently integrates strategic, operational and tactical headquarters and elements. It further establishes the need to effectively group capabilities under the appropriate command to best meet operational needs – coupled with the ability to rapidly shift these capabilities from one command to another to meet unforeseen or higher-priority commitments. The key is the allocation of mission-essential capabilities to operational and tactical commands, formations and units coupled with the ability to rapidly re-group and re-task capabilities between these entities as required.*

The issue of command centricity had its genesis in the CF's bureaucratic C2 process. Here, the concern was that, in the old NDHQ matrix, the responsibilities of commanders and staffs at all levels had become blurred, resulting in ineffectiveness and confusion. The sheer complexity of the staff processes made it difficult for executive leaders to influence the outcome, as the staff often seemed to be "working to some other agenda". In addition, strategic decisions were often taken by staff and direction given, with little recourse by the operational or tactical commander. Command centricity is intended to reassert the rightful place of commanders at the centre of the staff process, that is to ensure that the staff effort is guided by and focused on the commander's needs.

Such a philosophy is at the root of the CF's C2 doctrine that has been taught at staff colleges for years. Unfortunately, it has not been practiced. The term "command centric" in fact came from doctrine developed within the army, as it grappled with a revolution in C2 technology. In the simplest terms, it conceptually placed the commander at the centre of the information flow and made him the focus of all staff effort. In short, it ensured that all resources were harnessed to meet the commander's needs. Implicit in this was the traditional objective staff analysis, driven by the operational planning process (OPP) that would ensure that the commander was presented with the facts and the best possible analysis, options, risks and recommendations for action.

In implementing command centricity as a Transformation principle, two concerns have arisen. The first is directly related to understanding, as the term was, in some cases, interpreted as "commander" centric. This, it would appear, resulted in a belief in some quarters that because the commander said it or wanted it, it must be so. The result was a perceived reduction in objectivity and some indication of a growth of parochialism. This, then, led to an unwillingness to challenge commanders at lower levels about their decisions and actions.

The second issue relates to the limits of the application of the principle of command centricity. The command centric concept was developed for the operational environment where options need to be developed for tactical or operational problems, all under significant time constraints and with the authority for decisions vested in one person. It is a time-tested approach that works well in this context. Its application at the strategic level has merit, in particular where the issues are operational in nature. However, its application to the corporate environment, while attractive from the perspective of achieving simplicity and decisiveness, is questionable.

Decision-making in the corporate environment is shaped by two factors. First, it is usually dealing with a complex and often intractable problem for which there is no one, or even correct, answer. Second, the implementation of any solution normally requires the authority and support of a number of responsible actors. Given these factors, the most effective approach to reaching decisions is usually some form of collaborative process in which the expertise of each player is brought to the table in developing options and ultimately determining an acceptable solution. This, then, assures a general consensus amongst those with the authority to implement the solution. Unquestionably, such an approach is often much more time consuming but, in the long term, it ensures that workable solutions are agreed to and implemented.

Authorities, Responsibilities and Accountabilities. *Commanders must be provided with a clear articulation of their assigned authorities, responsibilities and accountabilities. In turn, commanders must ensure that they have a careful and comprehensive understanding of this direction and intent and that they, in turn, provide equivalent clarity in the provision of their guidance to their subordinate commanders.*

The issue of accountability is self-evident and, in recent years, has become a foundational principle within government and most large organizations. The one element that was new with the articulation of these principles was the explicit responsibility to ensure understanding of direction and intent. While this has always been understood, it is clear that the CDS, in developing his more devolved, command centric and mission command philosophy, needed to ensure such clarity.

Absent from this principle is any specific commentary on the issue of horizontal accountabilities. This is the situation increasingly found in large organizations in which responsibility or accountability cannot easily be apportioned to specific commanders. Here, we find situations where there needs to be some sharing of responsibility for achieving an objective, often across a large number of responsible actors. Again, it would appear that the principles are very much operationally focused and applied to a hierarchical organizational model. Clarity here is required.

Operational Focus. *Within the CF, operations and operational support take primacy over all other activities and considerations. This is a particular challenge at the strategic level in which departmental, corporate and CF priorities intersect; however, every strategic decision must be measured against the effect, positive or negative, that it will have on the CF's ability to effectively execute its assigned missions. Transformation initiatives that increase CF operational focus should be given the highest consideration.*

This principle is all about priorities and clearly states that operations are the CF's priority. Given the reality that the CF's purpose is operations, a fact that previously had sometimes become obscured, this made eminent sense. This principle has seen the re-emergence of a dominant operational culture within DND that is critical in achieving the overall cultural shift that the CDS expects. The only concern that should be expressed here is in the maintenance of balance. The focus at the strategic level must be out on the horizon, more concerned with shaping the environment tomorrow than the actions today. There is some indication in the application of this principle that, under the pressure of a high operational tempo, tomorrow is being neglected.

Mission Command. *The CF will continue to develop and exemplify mission command leadership – the leadership philosophy of the CF. In essence, mission command articulates the dynamic and decentralized execution of operations guided throughout by a clear articulation and understanding of the overriding commander's intent. This leadership concept demands the aggressive use of initiative at every level, a high degree of comfort in ambiguity and a tolerance for honest failure.*

Mission Command has been in practice within the CF for some years and, given the operational focus of Transformation, a logical principle to include. There continues to be some concern that the term is not fully understood, in particular with respect to the latitude subordinates are allowed. In practice, the philosophy should not limit a commander's control over subordinates, although there is some concern that this may be occurring. In addition, as with command centricity, there is a question as to how far the concept can be applied outside of the operational environment. Indeed, there is an argument that there are, or should be, two command philosophies, one for the operational sphere and one for the corporate. Bridging this divide based only on a mission command philosophy, without clarity on how the corporate environment should work, is a challenge.

An Integrated Regular, Reserve and Civilian CF. *Regular, reserve and civilian personnel will be more closely integrated into virtually every CF structure in order to ensure the best utilization of appropriate skills and experience at every level. In simple terms, what the individual can do is more important than from where he or she came or what uniform, if any, they wear.*

In some respects, this is an elaboration of the first principle. It takes the ideal of jointness further in endeavouring to remove all barriers between organizations and people. The principle is well articulated and easy to understand. Overcoming the cultural impediments to realizing it will take time.

ENDNOTES

1 John P. Kotter, *Leading Change* (Boston, MA: Harvard Business School Press, 1996).

2 Lieutenant-General (Retired) Michael Jeffery, "Inside Canadian Forces Transformation" *Canadian Military Journal*, 2010, in press.

3 Nicolo Machiavelli, *The Prince* (Florence, Italy: Antonio Blando d'Asola, 1532).

4 Currently named the North American Aerospace Defense Command.

5 A detailed review of the Paul Hellyer years and initiatives is available at Major-General Daniel Gosselin, "Hellyer's Ghosts: Unification of the Canadian Forces is 40 Years Old – Part One", *Canadian Military Journal*, Vol 9-2 (2008), 6-15. Part Two follows in Vol 9-3. Gosselin makes reference to the work of defence analyst Dr. Douglas Bland, Queen's University, which relates to unification and its consequences – D. Bland, *Canada's National Defence Volume 1: Defence Policy* (Kingston, Queen's University, School of Policy Studies, 1997); and D. Bland, *Chiefs of Defence: Government and the Unified Command of the Canadian Armed Forces* (Toronto: The Canadian Institute of Strategic Studies, 1995).

6 Proper titles for the Royal Canadian Navy, Canadian Army and Royal Canadian Air Force are capitalized. More generic references to a navy, army or air force, as in the amalgamated environments of the Canadian Forces, or as components of any foreign military, are not capitalized.

7 National Defence and CF Budgets 1999-2007 at <http://www.forces.gc.ca/site/Reports/budget05/back05_e.asp>.

8 Chief Review Services NDHQ 99: "Review of Restructuring and Re-engineering", February 2001 7050-10 (CRS).

9 The term "industrial age conflict" has been used for years, but it is best defined by General Sir Rupert Smith in *The Utility of Force: The Art of War in the Modern World* (New York, NY: Random House, 2007).

10 MND Reports on Change, at <http://www.dnd.ca/site/Minister/eng/Compendium/change2.htm>.

11 Maritime Command in Halifax, Mobile Command in Montreal and Air Command in Winnipeg.

12 Chief of the Maritime Staff (CMS), Chief of the Land Staff (CLS) and Chief of the Air Staff (CAS).

13 Department of National Defence, "Shaping the Future of the Canadian Forces: A Strategy for 2020", June 1999.

14 General Sir Rupert Smith, *The Utility of Force: The Art of War in the Modern World*. General Smith's assessment of the evolving conflict environment is but one of many. See also Colin S. Gray, *Another Bloody Century*; Colonel T. Hammes, *The Sling and the Stone*; and Mary Kaldor, *New and Old Wars: Organized Violence in a Global Era*.

15 Margaret Wheatley, *Leadership and the New Science: Discovering Order in a Chaotic World*. Third Edition (San Francisco: Berrett-Koehler Publishers, Inc., 2006); Michael Hammer and James Champy, *Reengineering the Corporation: A Manifesto for Business Revolution* (New York: HarperCollins Publishers, 1993).

16 Developed by the author.

17 Ibid

18 Ibid

19 Ronald Lippitt, Jeanne Watson and Bruce Westley, *Organizational Transformation: Approaches, Strategies, Theories* (Westport, CT: Praeger/Greenwood Publishing Group, 1958). The authors have distinguished between spontaneous or evolutionary change, fortuitous or accidental change and planned change. The first two types are unplanned. Unplanned change, according to their definition originates outside of the system experiencing change. Planned change on the other hand originates with a decision by the system to improve its functioning.

20 Gordon R. Sullivan and Michael V. Harper, *Hope is Not a Method: What Business Leaders Can Learn from America's Army* (Toronto, ON: Random House, 1996).

21 Edgar H. Schein, *Organizational Culture and Leadership* (San Francisco, CA: Jossey-Bass, 1992). As quoted in Brenda Bertrand, *Transformation within Organizational Culture: The Gap between Paper and Reality*. See weLEAD Inc., at <www.weLEADInLearning.org>.

22 John P. Kotter, *Leading Change*, 21. Kotter adapted this Exhibit 2 from Kotter, John P., "Why Transformation Efforts Fail," *Harvard Business Review* (March-April 1995), 61.

23 Prime Minister Paul Martin stated that Foreign Policy was one of the five pillars of his prime ministry, a subject about which he spoke at length during his tenure.

24 "Strategic Capability Investment Plan – Land Effect", 3136-5(CLS) dated 26 June 2003, the letter written by then-Lieutenant-General Hillier while Chief of the Land Staff, 2003.

25 As the newly elected leader of the Liberal Party (November 2003), Prime Minister Paul Martin articulated his new vision for Canadian foreign policy, including enhanced international leadership for Canada while contributing to new thinking about how the international community governs itself. See Paul Martin's government's International *Policy Review*, 2004.

26 CDS tasks for the new Chief of Transformation (CT), then-Major-General Walter Natynczyk, were broadcast through CANFORGEN 098/05 CDS 045/05 301137Z MAY 05, "CF Transformation Team Created / CDS Action Team Update", 30 May 2005.

27 In common military usage, the number of stars denotes the commissioned officer rank or level - (one-star – Brigadier-General or Commodore; two-star – Major-General or Rear Admiral; three-star – Lieutenant-General or Vice-Admiral; four-star – General or Admiral.)

28 SJS Concept of Operations – Briefing to Command Council, 29 June 2006.

29 The term, "decade of darkness", was coined as the title of a report that focused on the capacity of the CF to respond to government direction. However, it is often used out of context of the report. See G. E. (Joe) Sharpe and Allan D. English, *The Decade of Darkness* (Kingston, ON: Canadian Forces Leadership Institute, 2003.)

30 Alan Okros, "Understanding the Decade of Darkness", a paper presented at the University of Calgary Conference, *Forced to Change – Education and Reforms Ten Years After* (Toronto, ON: Canadian Forces College, 2008.)

31 The Prime Minister generated a Cabinet shuffle on 14 August 2007 that saw the Honourable Gordon O'Connor replaced as MND by the Honourable Peter MacKay.

32 Lieutenant-General (Retired) Ray R. Crabbe, Vice-Admiral (Retired) Lynn G. Mason and Lieutenant-General (Retired) Fred R. Sutherland, *A Report on the Validation of the Transformed Canadian Forces Command Structure*, 31 January 2007; and Lieutenant-General (Retired) Ray R. Crabbe, Vice-Admiral (Retired) Lynn G. Mason and Lieutenant-General (Retired) Fred R. Sutherland, *A Report on the Impact of Canadian Forces Transformation on Defence Strategic Enablers*, 5 September 2007.

33 The CDS' Transformation Missile, a schematic first used by General Hillier in his Transformation briefing at the General and Flag Officers Seminar, Spring 2007, after having visited Vimy Ridge in April. Later in 2007, the schematic was conceptualized in greater detail by the Chief of Force Development, and titled "Action Areas to Transform the Force for Effect."

34 General Sir Rupert Smith, *The Utility of Force: The Art of War in the Modern World*, p. 271, summarizes the kind of conflict faced in the 21st Century with a framework of six basic trends:

- The ends for which we fight are changing from the hard objectives that decide a political outcome to those of establishing conditions in which the outcome may be decided;
- We fight amongst the people not on the battlefield;
- Conflicts tend to be timeless, even unending;
- We fight so as to preserve the force rather than risking all to gain the objective;
- On each occasion new uses are found for old weapons and organizations that are the products of industrial war; and
- The sides are mostly non-state, comprising some form of multi-national grouping against some non-state party or parties.

35 General Charles C. Krulak, "The Strategic Corporal: Leadership in the Three Block War", *Marines Magazine*, January 1999. The "three block war" is a concept devised by General Krulak in the late 1990s to describe the complex spectrum of challenges likely to be faced by soldiers on the modern battlefield. In three contiguous city blocks, soldiers may be required to conduct full-scale combat, peace support operations, and humanitarian relief.

36 DND, CDS Action Team (CAT 1) Final Report – CF C2, (1950-9 (CAT 1)), 29 June 2005.

37 As an example, in 1999, during the planning for Operation ABACUS, the environments could not agree on the meaning of "command and control" terminology even though it was accepted NATO doctrine. (The author documenting this was the JTF Commander for Op ABACUS.)

38 "The Way Ahead for the Canadian Forces", CDS Transformation Brief addresses the vision, key enablers, force structure, etc., (see slide 27/32), (Ottawa, National Defence Headquarters, 2005). Referenced in Major-General Daniel Gosselin, "Hellyer's Ghosts: Unification of the Canadian Forces is 40 Years Old - Part One", *Canadian Military Journal*, Vol 9-2 (2008), 6-15.

39 "The Way Ahead for the Canadian Forces", ibid.

40 "9/11 changed the paradigm. Before you spend any money, you've got to have an understanding as to what kind of military force you want. Our budgets are quite restricted. We only have so much money. We're not going to spend money we don't have. Yes, I do believe eventually there will be increases in defence spending. But they're only going to be taken when we're absolutely convinced that this is the right

way to go". Prime Minister Paul Martin, in response to questions from the media, Press Conference, 12 December 2003.

41 Interestingly, there is some anecdotal evidence to suggest that the greatest resistance to the SCTF came from within the navy where the idea of amphibious warfare was treated with suspicion. It was seen by some as a wasteful distraction from the "real" role of the navy – the protection of US carrier battle groups.

42 CDS, *Transformation*, revised Vision Statement, October 2007, following feedback from senior officers at the CDS G/FO Seminar, May 2007. .

43 In *Leading Change*, p. 57, author John P. Kotter refers to the importance of a "guiding coalition" and identifies four characteristics essential for its effectiveness: position of power, expertise, credibility and leadership.

44 The Executive Leadership Team consists of those executives who share the responsibility for governance and stewardship of the organization. In the context of the CF, this implies the CDS' direct subordinates and encompasses the membership of Armed Forces Council and Commanders Council. It should also include the DND executives as defined by membership in Defence Management Committee.

45 There are many interpretations as to the nature and importance of coherence within organizations and, in particular, in those undergoing organizational change. A very generic description of strategic coherence is presented here, but clearly there are many other definitions. See "Management Control and Coherence: Some Unresolved Questions", Research Centre, Business School Paris, ESSEC (École supérieure des sciences économiques et commerciales), a Working Paper, May 2003.

46 *A Report on the Validation of the Transformed Canadian Forces Command Structure*, 31 January 2007.

47 To "picket and bypass" is a tactical term whereby advancing troops bypass pockets of enemy resistance but leave troops to observe the position to ensure that any enemy action is known. Such an approach is taken to avoid becoming engaged in operations that may slow down the advance or even jeopardize achievement of the objective.

48 In *Leading Change*, John P. Kotter emphasizes that creating a sense of urgency is critical to moving the institution forward. Thus, the longer the change leader spends in preparation, the less likely that a sense of urgency will be achieved.

49 DND/CF, *Canada First Defence Strategy* (CFDS), Backgrounder, 12 May 2008, "The future security environment calls for a combat-capable, flexible, multi-role military.

Recognizing this, the Canada First Defence Strategy sets out a vision for future operations as well as the funding required to support it. This vision, coupled with committed long-term funding, will allow the Canadian Forces to maintain excellence in operations at home, be a solid partner in continental defence, and fulfill a leadership role abroad." Available at <www.forces.gc.ca>.

50 Robert S. Kaplan and David P. Norton, "Strategic Management: An Emerging Profession," *Balanced Scorecard Report*, Vol 6, Number 3, May-June, 2004. A number of change management references agree, indicating that most change attempts fail in execution.

51 "The Way Ahead for the Canadian Forces", see slide 30/32 on integrated CF efforts (vision vs. resources).

52 1905-1(CFTT) "Direction to Functional Review Working Groups", 22 March 2007.

53 CDS SITREP 02/05 September 2005.

54 *A Report on the Validation of the Transformed Canadian Forces Command Structure* and *A Report on the Impact of Canadian Forces Transformation on Defence Strategic Enablers.*

55 Douglas L. Bland, *Chiefs of Defence: Government and the Unified Command of the Canadian Armed Forces* (Toronto, ON: Canadian Institute of Strategic Studies, 1995), 291.

ABOUT THE AUTHOR

LIEUTENANT-GENERAL (RETIRED) MICHAEL K. JEFFERY, CMM, CD

Lieutenant-General Mike Jeffery joined the Royal Regiment of Canadian Artillery in 1964 under the Canadian Army Soldier Apprentice Program. He was commissioned in 1967.

During a military career that spanned 39 years, he served in a variety of command and staff appointments both in Canada and overseas. Through the 1990s, Lieutenant-General Jeffery served in a number of positions within the CF and the army, intimately involved with organizational change. This included a period as Chief of the Land Staff during which time he helped develop and implement a strategy of change within the army.

Lieutenant-General Jeffery retired from regular service in August 2003.

SELECTED READINGS

Bland, Douglas L., *Chiefs of Defence: Government and the Unified Command of the Canadian Armed Forces*, (Toronto: Canadian Institute of Strategic Studies, 1995).

Bridges, William, *Managing Transitions: Making the Most of Change*, (Reading, MA: Addison-Wesley Publishing, 1991).

Covey, Stephen R., *Principle Centered Leadership*, (New York, NY: Fireside, 1990).

Hammer, Michael, and James Champy, *Reengineering the Corporation: A Manifesto for Business Revolution*, (New York, NY: Harper Collins, 1993).

Hughes, Richard L. and Katherine C. Beatty, *Becoming a Strategic Leader*, (San Francisco, CA: Jossey-Bass and Center for Creative Leadership, 2005).

Kotter, John, *Leading Change*, (Boston, MA: Harvard Business School, 1996).

MacGregor, Douglas A., *Breaking the Phalanx: A New Design for Landpower in the 21st Century*, (Westport, CT: Praeger Publishers, 1997).

Owens, Admiral Bill, *Lifting the Fog of War*, (New York, NY: Farrar, Straus and Giroux, 2000).

Peters, Tom, and Nancy Austin, *A Passion for Excellence: The Leadership Difference*, (New York, NY: Warner Books, 1985).

Schein, Edgar H., *Organisational Culture and Leadership*, 2nd edition, (San Francisco, CA: Jossey-Bass, 1992).

Smith, General Sir Rupert, *The Utility of Force: The Art of War in the Modern World*, (New York, NY: Random House, 2007).

Sullivan, Gordon R. and Michael V. Harper, *Hope is Not a Method: What Business Leaders Can Learn from America's Army*, (Toronto, ON: Random House, 1996).

Government of Canada/Department of National Defence Reports

7050-10 (CRS) – Chief Review Services NDHQ 99: *Review of Restructuring and Re-Engineering*, February 2001.

1950-9 (CAT 1) – CDS Action Team 1 (CAT 1) Final Report – CF C2, 29 June 2005.

1950-9 (CAT 2) – CDS Action Team 2 (CAT 2) Final Report – Concepts for Integrated Force Development, Integrated Force Generation, and Coalition Advocacy, 30 June 2005.

CDS Action Team 3 (CAT 3) Interim Report – Operational Capabilities, 25 July 2005.

CDS Action Team 4 (CAT 4) Final Report – Institutional Alignment, 6 July 2005.

1950-9 (CT) – CDS Planning Guidance – CF Transformation, 18 October 2005.

1950-2-4 (CFTT/DTP) – Concept of Operations: Strategic Command, 18 October 2005.

Canada's International Policy Statement: *A Role of Pride and Influence in the World – Defence*, 2005, at <www.international.gc.ca> and <www.forces. gc.ca>.

A Report on the Validation of the Transformed Canadian Forces Command Structure, by Lieutenant-General (Retired) Ray R. Crabbe, Vice-Admiral (Retired) Lynn G. Mason and Lieutenant-General (Retired) Fred R. Sutherland, 31 January 2007.

A Report on the Impact of Canadian Forces Transformation on Defence Strategic Enablers, by Lieutenant-General (Retired) Ray R Crabbe, Vice-Admiral (Retired) Lynn G. Mason and Lieutenant-General (Retired) Fred R. Sutherland, 05 September 2007.

GLOSSARY

Glossary definitions for concepts incorporated into this book are those provided in the CF manual, *Leadership in the Canadian Forces: Conceptual Foundations* and *Leadership in the Canadian Forces: Leading the Institution.*

Command

The authority vested in an individual of the armed forces for the direction, coordination, and control of military forces. Also, the authority-based process of planning, organizing, leading, and controlling the efforts of subordinates and the use of other military resources to achieve military goals. (See *management*).

Commander's Intent

The commander's personal expression of why one is conducting an operation and what one hopes to achieve. It is a clear and concise statement of the desired end-state and acceptable risk. Its strength is the fact that it allows subordinates to exercise initiative in the absence of orders, when unexpected opportunities arise, or when the original concept of operations no longer applies.

Culture

A shared and relatively stable pattern of behaviours, values, and assumptions that a group has learned over time as an effective means of maintaining internal social stability and adapting to its environment, and that are transmitted to new members as the correct ways to perceive, think, and act in relation to these issues.

Distributed Leadership

The idea, first, that the capacity for leadership is not limited to people selected for and assigned to senior positions of responsibility and authority but, in varying degrees, is broadly distributed throughout the CF population, and, second, that the function of leadership should be shared. Bringing out this potential requires a combination of broadly based leader skill development, opportunities for junior leaders to lead and emergent leaders to step forward, professional cohesion across the leadership team, and a culture that supports and rewards initiative and sensible risk-taking.

Executive Leadership

The overseeing of responsibilities and the coordinating of capacities for operational success. Executive leaders require a broader knowledge and understanding of the context of the organization. They execute and interpret the leader's vision by articulating a plan of action that includes directing the work of others, negotiating strategies, allocating resources, planning and monitoring activities, promoting ethical climate, and setting goals and practices needed to sustain and improve the CF as an institution.

Institution

A formally established organization with a specific professional function to perform consistently over time. An institution has legal or quasi-legal standing and permanence. Institutions dependent upon bureaucracy and hierarchy are generally slow to adapt and change, while networked institutions organized around professional ideals are more adaptable to changing circumstances.

Institutional Leaders

Officers, non-commissioned officers, and members of the Department of National Defence who, by virtue of their rank, position and/or responsibilities, have significant influence on CF members and on the development or implementation of CF policy, and/or represent the CF within the domestic and international security environment.

Institutional Leadership

The process of directly or indirectly shaping the reputation and effectiveness of the CF by means of formal authority or personal influence.

Leadership (Generic)

The process of directly or indirectly influencing others, by means of formal authority or personal attributes, to act in accordance with one's intent or a shared purpose.

Leadership (Effective CF Leadership)

The process of "directing, motivating and enabling others to accomplish the mission professionally and ethically, while developing or improving capabilities that contribute to mission success." This definition reflects that leadership roles in the CF exist to serve CF effectiveness, i.e., the extent to which stated objectives are achieved. In any definition of effectiveness, the achievement of objectives may be qualified by other criteria, such as efficiency or lawfulness. The CF effectiveness framework identifies mission success as the primary objective, with member well-being and commitment, internal integration, and external adaptability as enabling or supporting objectives.

Learning Organization

An organization that is able, on an ongoing basis, to critically examine its performance, assimilate information from the environment, and transform itself, with a view to adapting to challenges and positioning itself to exploit opportunities or to establish a dominant capability.

Management

The authority-based process of planning, organizing, leading, and controlling the efforts of organizational members and the use of other organizational resources to achieve organizational goals. (See *command*).

Military Ethos

The living spirit that creates and shapes military culture, finds full expression through the conduct of members of the profession of arms, and comprises three fundamental components: beliefs and expectations about military service, Canadian values, and Canadian military values.

Military Strategy

The bridge that cements military power to political purposes and comprises numerous dimensions related to people and politics, preparation for conflict, and war and conflict.

Mission Command

A command philosophy that promotes decentralized decision-making, freedom and speed of action, and initiative. It entails three enduring tenets: the importance of understanding a superior commander's intent, a clear responsibility to fulfil that intent, and timely decision-making. To exercise mission command, a commander must give orders in a manner that ensures subordinates understand his or her intent, their own tasks and the context of those tasks; tell subordinates what effect they are to achieve and the reasons why it needs achieving; allocate appropriate resources to carry out missions and tasks; and allow subordinates to decide within their delegated freedom of action how best to achieve their missions and tasks.

Professional Ideology

A framework guiding the profession of arms that claims specialist, theory-based knowledge and a commitment to the ethical values that guide the application of that knowledge.

Professionalism

In general, the display of the qualities or features of a profession. With respect to the CF, professionalism means that CF members apply their unique body of military expertise in accordance with the civic, legal, ethical and military values of the military ethos, pursuant to the profession's responsibility to society, and to a strong personal identification with military activities and the military way of life.

Senior Leader

This concept is not tied to doctrinal definitions of senior officer and senior non-commissioned member. Rather, it describes leaders who have developed the proficiency and the leader attributes that allow them to operate at the institutional and/or strategic level and to influence the effectiveness of the CF and the culture of the institution.

Stewardship

The special obligation of officers and non-commissioned members who by virtue of their rank or appointment are directly concerned with ensuring that the profession of arms in Canada fulfils its organizational and professional responsibilities to the CF and Canada, including the use of their power and influence to ensure the continued development of the institution, its cultures and its future leaders to meet the expectations of Canadians.

Strategy

See *military strategy*.

Systems Thinking

A way of thinking about and diagnosing problems that intentionally avoids compartmentalized analysis in favour of considering problem symptoms in relation to broad process interactions and system-wide effects. A discipline with various frameworks, spanning the physical and social sciences, engineering and management, for seeing wholes, interrelationships and patterns of change.

Three-block War

An operational contingency in which military personnel may be confronted by the entire spectrum of tactical challenges in the same area of operation, ranging from humanitarian assistance to peacekeeping and/or to combat, all in the same day and all within three city blocks.

Transactional Leadership

A general pattern of influence based on the provision of various rewards or benefits in exchange for extra effort or improved performance; sometimes discussed with reference to principles of economic exchange.

Transformational Leadership

A pattern of leader influence intended to alter the characteristics of individuals, organizations, or societies in a fairly dramatic or substantial way so that they are somehow more accomplished, or better equipped to deal with the challenges they face, or are likely to face.

Visioning

The art and practice of developing an imagined possibility for the future that moves beyond current capability and provides an intellectual bridge from today to tomorrow in a manner that establishes a basis for positive action, growth, and transformation.

ACRONYMS

9/11	The 11 September 2001 Terrorism Attack on the World Trade Towers in New York
ADM	Assistant Deputy Minister
AFC	Armed Forces Council
C2	Command and Control
Canada Com	Canada Command
CANOSCOM	Canadian Operational Support Command
CANSOFCOM	Canadian Special Operations Forces Command
CAS	Chief of the Air Staff
CAT	CDS Action Team(s)
CDA	Canadian Defence Academy
CDI	Chief of Defence Intelligence
CDS	Chief of the Defence Staff
CEFCOM	Canadian Expeditionary Forces Command
CF	Canadian Forces
CFD	Chief of Force Development
CFDS	Canada First Defence Strategy
CFLI	Canadian Forces Leadership Institute
CFTT	Canadian Forces Transformation Team
CLS	Chief of the Land Staff
CMS	Chief of the Maritime Staff
CONOPS	Concept of Operations
COO	Concept of Operations
COS	Chief of Staff
CProg	Chief of Programme
CRS	Chief of Review Services
CT	Chief of Transformation
DART	Disaster Assistance Response Team
DCDS	Deputy Chief of the Defence Staff
DCP	Defence Capabilities Plan
DGSP	Director General Strategic Planning
DM	Deputy Minister
DND	Department of National Defence
DOS	Director of Staff
DPS	Defence Policy Statement

ECS	Environmental Chiefs of Staff (maritime, land, air)
FD	Force Development
FE	Force Employment
FG	Force Generation
G/FO	General and Flag Officers
GWOT	Global War on Terrorism
IMRS	Integrated Managed Readiness System
ISAF	(NATO-led) International Security Assistance Force
JTF	Joint Task Force
JTF North	Joint Task Force North
JTF2	Joint Task Force 2
JTFA	Joint Task Force Atlantic
LDF	Leadership Development Framework
LGen	Lieutenant-General
MCCRT	Management, Command and Control Re-engineering Team
MCDV	Maritime Coastal Defence Vessel
MGen	Major-General
MND	Minister of National Defence
MND SW	Multinational Division Southwest
MSTF	Mission-Specific Task Force
NATO	North Atlantic Treaty Organisation
NCM	Non-commissioned members
NDHQ	National Defence Headquarters
NORAD	Previously North American Air Defense, currently North American Aerospace Defense Command
OEF	Operation ENDURING FREEDOM
OIF	Operation IRAQI FREEDOM
OPP	Operational planning process
PA	Public affairs
PDF	Professional Development Framework
PM	Prime Minister

SCONDVA	Standing Committee on National Defence and Veterans Affairs
SCTF	Standing Contingency Task Force
SFOR	(NATO) Stabilization Force
SITREP	Situational report
SJS	Strategic Joint Staff
SOF	Special Operations Forces
SOG	Special Operations Group
ToR	Terms of Reference
TSAT	Transformation Staff Action Team
TSG	Transformation Steering Group
UN	United Nations
UNITAF	Unified Task Force
UNPROFOR	United Nations Protection Force
US	United States
VCDS	Vice-Chief of the Defence Staff

INDEX